D1133571

Cultivating Careers:
Professional Development
for Campus IT

Cynthia Golden, Editor

ISBN 0-9672853-5-6
©2006 EDUCAUSE. Available electronically at
www.educause.edu/cultivatingcareers

An EDUCAUSE *e-Book*

Cultivating Careers: Professional Development for Campus IT

Foreword
by Susan E. Metros, The Ohio State University

Preface: A Commitment to Professional Development
by Cynthia Golden, EDUCAUSE

Acknowledgments
by Cynthia Golden, EDUCAUSE

Part I: The Organizational Perspective

Chapter 1: **Perspectives on IT Leadership**
by James D. Bruce, MIT, and Brian McDonald, MOR Associates, Inc.

Chapter 2: **A Comprehensive Approach to Professional Development for an IT Staff**
by Gene Spencer and Jeannie Zappe, Bucknell University

Chapter 3: **Organizational Strategies for Fostering a Culture of Learning**
by Marilu Goodyear, Kathleen Ames-Oliver, and Keith Russell, University of Kansas

ISBN 0-9672853-5-6

©2006 EDUCAUSE. Available electronically at
www.educause.edu/cultivatingcareers

An EDUCAUSE *e-Book*

Foreword

In 2004, the EDUCAUSE Center for Applied Research (ECAR) published a research study titled *Information Technology Leadership in Higher Education: The Condition of the Community.*[1] While many of the 2,000 information technology professionals surveyed agreed that IT leaders were effective in their positions, higher education was a calling, and universities were a good place to work, they were concerned about dwindling interest in leadership positions. The survey found fewer candidates in the pipeline than needed to fill expected vacancies, with a quarter of all respondents considering retirement within five years. In addition, the data showed that the current IT leadership community lacks both gender and racial diversity. The report concluded that in order to retain and "grow" current staff and to attract newcomers to the profession and to leadership positions, the IT community must provide its workforce with targeted professional development and mentoring opportunities.

EDUCAUSE, a nonprofit association of more than 2,000 colleges, universities, and educational organizations whose mission is to advance higher education by promoting the intelligent use of information technology, takes the continuity, growth, and diversity of the higher education IT workforce seriously. The association's leaders charged its Professional Development Committee to advise EDUCAUSE staff on the development and delivery of a suite of resources aimed at supporting their membership's work and advancing their professional careers. These opportunities range from conferences, seminars, institutes, targeted leadership training events, fellowship, scholarship, and volunteer opportunities to a wealth of easily accessible presentations and publications.

The idea for this book, *Cultivating Careers: Professional Development for Campus IT,* was conceived by EDUCAUSE Vice President Cynthia Golden, who is responsible for coordinating the content of the association's professional development activities, as well as content and knowledge management initiatives. She understood that while there exists a plethora of books published on leadership, and many dedicated to leadership within corporate IT operations, there were limited resources targeted toward IT professional development in general and aspiring IT leaders in higher education in particular. One notable exception is

©2006 Susan E. Metros

Technology Everywhere: A Campus Agenda for Educating and Managing Workers in the Digital Age.[2] This collection of essays addresses recruiting, hiring, and training knowledge worker professionals and educating IT learners to manage the ever-increasing flow of information. It serves as a foundation for many of the concepts in *Cultivating Careers.*

Cultivating Careers addresses the needs of our IT workforce community by providing an overview of current and emerging professional development practices and opportunities, focusing on aspects of the profession that are unique to higher education. It provides how-to approaches both from individual and organizational perspectives and is interspersed with ideas and examples that can be replicated on campuses both big and small, private and public. The authors are leaders from a variety of institutions, including large research universities and small liberal arts colleges. They are CIOs, librarians, technology directors, faculty members, and professional organization leaders. In the pages that follow, they share their experiences, wisdom, and lessons learned.

This book is written for those responsible for managing and leading information services organizations in colleges and universities. It is designed to serve as a guide both for those who have responsibility for preparing the next generation of leaders and for those who aspire to or have recently assumed greater responsibility and leadership in higher education. While the title of this book refers to campus information technology, it is intended to serve a broad segment of the higher education population. It is important to recognize that at many institutions, IT and library organizations have merged, and distributed IT service units work in concert with central IT groups to provide customer support. All professional personnel within these organizations share a need for professional development and thus constitute the audience for this book's content.

Those of us who have had the good fortune to work in this rapidly changing world of IT in higher education have an obligation to prepare the next generation to support and to lead higher education into the future. It is my expectation, and the expectation of the EDUCAUSE Professional Development Committee, that *Cultivating Careers: Professional Development for Campus IT* will serve as a guide for today's leaders to help prepare our workforce for tomorrow's challenges and to entice and inspire those beginning their careers to actively seek rewarding leadership opportunities in higher education.

—*Susan E. Metros*
Chair, EDUCAUSE Professional Development Committee, 2004 and 2005

Endnotes

1. Richard N. Katz and Gail Salaway, "Information Technology Leadership in Higher Education: The Condition of the Community Key Findings" (Boulder, Colo.: EDUCAUSE Center for Applied Research, January 2004), <http://www.educause.edu/LibraryDetailPage/666?ID=EKF0401>.

2. Brian Hawkins, Julia A. Rudy, and William H. Wallace, Jr., eds., *Technology Everywhere: A Campus Agenda for Educating and Managing Workers in the Digital Age*, EDUCAUSE Leadership Strategies Series, vol. 6 (San Francisco: Jossey-Bass, 2002), <http://www.educause.edu/LibraryDetailPage/666?ID=PUB7006>.

Preface: A Commitment to Professional Development

In the past few years, I have had the opportunity to think more broadly about the condition of the higher education information technology community, the changing nature of IT, the role of leaders in IT, and how those of us in this community prepare ourselves and others—both to support the changing needs of our colleges and universities and to advance in our careers. The success of our institutions—and our IT organizations—depends on our people and how well prepared they are to meet the challenges that lie ahead.

IT continues to have a profound impact on higher education, influencing not only almost every aspect of a student's life—from performing library research to interacting with professors to dating and doing laundry—but also almost every campus function. (Nowhere was this more evident than during the Y2K remediation process, where we learned, at some institutions for the first time, the depth and breadth of dependence on IT.) The evolving global digital network has fundamentally changed the nature of our communications, across campus and around the world. The rapid advances in processing power, data-storage capacity, bandwidth, and software development have revolutionized research, teaching, and learning. And our Net Gen students, who have grown up with technology and have never known life without the Internet, have expectations for IT access, mobility, and convenience that have huge implications for teaching, learning, and institutional services.[1]

Those of us who have been in the IT business in higher education for more than a few years have seen dramatic changes over a relatively short time and have witnessed the effects of these changes on the IT organization. In talking about the evolution of the IT organization, Polley McClure, vice president and CIO at Cornell University, noted: "Growth of this magnitude has necessarily strained many fronts. As IT has forced its way into all facets of our institutions, it has displaced other priorities and caused us to change the way everyone on campus works. It has spawned entirely new academic disciplines. It has opened new approaches and ideas in almost every field."[2]

©2006 Cynthia Golden

It's All About the People

Many IT organizational structures now mirror the complexity of the technologies we support, in stark contrast to the early days of campus computing, when the central "computer center" staff ran the mainframe and worked with a few faculty on research projects. Today, centralized IT service departments work with distributed IT staff in colleges, schools, and departments to provide a multifaceted web of services.

The 2004 EDUCAUSE Core Data Service (http://www.educause.edu/apps/coredata/), which includes an annual survey that collects data about technology environments and practices at U.S. institutions, reported that our colleges and universities have an average of 60.5 FTE staff in IT, but the actual numbers range from one IT person at a small bachelor of arts/liberal arts institution to a high of 652 IT staff at a doctoral-extensive university. On average across all types of institutions, 83.5 percent of IT staff members are housed within a central group; the remaining 17.5 percent are disbursed throughout the organization. The number of distributed/departmental staff increases at a significant rate as the complexity of the institution increases. IT organizations at smaller or less well-funded institutions struggle to support these same complex services with bare-bones staff. At these institutions, staff often wear multiple hats, and even those with manager/director or CIO titles can be very hands-on.[3] No matter the size or type of institution or the complexity of the organization, all face similar challenges when it comes to helping staff members stay current within their respective areas of specialty, keep up with the changes in technology, develop new skills or improve current skills, and develop a broader awareness of the role the staff and the department play in supporting the mission of the institution.

Making a case for professional development (PD) is easy. Simply stated, an investment in our people is an investment in our institutions and in our individual and collective future. Our colleges and universities reap the benefit of the development of staff, usually in a very direct way. Staff with current skills are more effective at analyzing and solving problems, are better equipped to complete projects accurately and on time, and can do a better job in providing effective technology support to the community. Research indicates that an organization's commitment to staff development is directly linked not only to increased productivity but also to high staff loyalty. Both the recruitment and the retention of employees can be greatly improved with an ongoing staff-development program.[4]

Actually making PD happen is harder. An old slogan from CAUSE, one of the parent organizations of EDUCAUSE, stated: "Professional Development Is Everyone's Responsibility." That quote appeared on mouse pads and notepads for many years, and it bears repeating today. Although the IT unit is responsible for encouraging staff development, planning specific strategies, and providing funds for training, the individual must take an equal or greater interest in his or her own personal growth.

If we recognize that ongoing PD—essentially, lifelong learning—is critical to our survival and success as individuals, we can work in partnership with our institutions to achieve mutual benefits. Supervisors, acting as coaches and mentors, can work with staff to build PD plans that include formal training and informal exploration. Supervisors can introduce staff to professional communities of learners and can assign projects that will allow them to grow and to be challenged. But the staff member has to meet the supervisor at least halfway. He or she must take the initiative to investigate opportunities, demonstrate an interest in the profession, and be willing to invest his or her own time in these endeavors.

Time and Money

How do we combat the problem that there never seems to be enough time or enough money to spend on PD?

At one of my former institutions, we used to joke within the educational technology group that we were the "victims of our own success." We worked hard to spread the word about technology—to show the faculty just what was possible and how technology could support their teaching and their students' learning. We were so successful in spreading the word that in a very short time, the demand for our services quickly outstripped the abilities of the staff to meet them. One of the side effects of our newfound success was that our workload made it extremely difficult to set aside the time for classes, conferences, presentations, or writing—PD tasks were consistently pushed to the bottom of the job list. Although the group members had a strong sense of intellectual curiosity and were quick to pick up "the next big thing," taking the time to engage in formal planning, and then taking the time to attend a conference or other event, seemed impossible. The solution to this lack of time, of course, is to force the time. Putting an appointment on the calendar for professional planning between staff and supervisors and then keeping that appointment constitutes a first step.

As for money, the 2004 Core Data Service survey revealed that higher education spends, on average, $1,123 per year per IT staff member on professional development or training. This amount is relatively constant across all Carnegie classifications with the exception of baccalaureate schools, which invest significantly more in the development of their staff than do doctoral and comprehensive universities and associate degree–granting colleges. The average amount also remained consistent from 2003 to 2004.[5] Having a budget line item for staff development places importance on investing in staff. For those of us struggling with funding PD activities, we can use a little creativity and thoughtfulness to take advantage of regional and local opportunities and to implement strategies that encourage people to share what they have learned.[6] We can also benefit from the very effective PD opportunities available through online communities and networking and through campus and local events.

The Role of IT Leaders

As our institutions are challenged to embrace the extraordinary opportunities that evolving technologies bring to higher education, our IT organizations are challenged to provide leadership and guidance for the strategic investment in IT, as well as day-to-day support for the basic functions of IT. Those who lead the IT organizations, and those who aspire to do so, must understand *and develop* the evolving set of skills required to obtain and to succeed in these roles. In a 2004 EDUCAUSE Center for Advanced Research (ECAR) study survey, more than a quarter of the 1,850 respondents, who included senior IT leaders, planned to leave higher education within the next five years, and only 157 respondents indicated that they aspired to these soon-to-be-vacated positions.[7] Preparation of the next generation of IT leaders has become critical.

Brian Hawkins and Deanna Marcum pointed out that leaders of any IT unit on campus must be active participants in the management of the academic enterprise, that they must be true partners in achieving this mission of the institution, and that they must move from playing the role of a specialist to that of a generalist.[8] A 2005 ECAR research bulletin indicated that although the development of leadership skills may be overlooked in many staff-development programs, in IT professional development there is another void specific to higher education—"how to imbue an understanding of how higher education's history, organizational structure, governance, and practices impact IT."[9] As IT leaders move away from being viewed as "just" technology experts and toward playing a key role in the operation and strategic direction of the institution, the understanding of governance, budgets, and values of higher education becomes critical.

IT leaders, and those who aspire to these positions, can have significant influence on the PD strategies of their units and on the development of a culture of lifelong learning. Working in partnership with human resource offices, consultants, and staff, and leading by example, the IT leader can help create a climate of success and an expectation that people will continue to grow and develop in their fields. A former IT leader at MIT told his staff that every year they would "raise the bar"—expecting that his staff would achieve more than they had the year before. The expectation simply became part of the culture.

What Works

This book is full of first-person experiences, practical advice, and real-world examples of what works—what tactics are successful—in the implementation of a PD program. Part I, "The Organizational Perspective," opens with a chapter by James Bruce and Brian McDonald on the changing nature of IT leadership and the evolving broader skill sets required of today's and tomorrow's leaders. In chapter 2, Gene Spencer and Jeannie Zappe outline a comprehensive approach to PD for IT staff. Marilu Goodyear, Kathleen Ames-Oliver, and Keith Russell explain organizational strategies for fostering a culture of learning in chapter 3. The next five chapters compose Part II, "The Individual Perspective." David Dodd and William Hogue give advice in chapter 4 on how staff can take control of their careers. In chapter 5, Catherine Yang and Susan Metros stress the importance of both having and being a mentor. Daniel Updegrove and I, in chapter 6, talk about getting involved in the profession and the personal and professional rewards that can bring. In chapter 7, Tracey Leger-Hornby and Ronald Bleed offer insights into achieving a work/life balance. In chapter 8, Brian Hawkins writes about skills and habits that lead to becoming a successful and effective IT professional. Finally, in chapter 9, Lida Larsen and I use both the organizational and the individual perspective to discuss building our workforce for the future and the preparation of the next generation of IT leaders.

Summary

Having strong PD programs in place is key to effectively supporting the mission of our colleges and universities. As members of the higher education community, we are each responsible for making that professional development happen. Ideally, the expectation that we are constantly learning and are actively involved in our own development can become part of our organizational cultures. To best support our institutions, we have to invest in people. We must accept the responsibility and take the initiative to ensure that each staff member actively participates in both formal and informal activities that will enhance his or her skills and professional marketability. Doing this requires time and resources, but mostly, it requires commitment on the part of the institution and the individual.

—Cynthia Golden
Vice President, EDUCAUSE

Endnotes

1. Diana G. Oblinger and James L. Oblinger, eds., *Educating the Net Generation*, e-book (Boulder, Colo.: EDUCAUSE, 2005), <http://www.educause.edu/books/educatingthenetgen/5989>.

2. Polley A. McClure, "Managing the Complexity of Campus Information Resources," in *Organizing and Managing Information Resources on Your Campus*, Polley A. McClure, ed. (San Francisco: Jossey-Bass, 2003), pp. 1–14, <http://www.educause.edu/ir/library/pdf/pub7007c.pdf>.

3. The EDUCAUSE Core Data Service <http://www.educause.edu/apps/coredata/> is available to participating EDUCAUSE members; the annual summary report is publicly available.

4. Allison F. Dolan, "Recruiting, Retaining, and Reskilling Campus IT Professionals," in *Technology Everywhere: A Campus Agenda for Educating and Managing Workers in the Digital Age*, Brian L. Hawkins, Julia A. Rudy, and William H. Wallace, Jr., eds., EDUCAUSE Leadership Strategies Series, vol. 6 (San Francisco: Jossey-Bass, 2002), pp. 75–91, <http://www.educause.edu/ir/library/pdf/pub7006h.pdf>.

5. EDUCAUSE Core Data Service, op. cit.

6. Paul Gandel and Cynthia Golden, "Professional Development in Tough Financial Times," *EDUCAUSE Quarterly*, vol. 27, no. 1 (2004), <http://www.educause.edu/LibraryDetail/666?ID=EQM0416>.

7. Richard N. Katz et al., *Information Technology Leadership in Higher Education: The Condition of the Community* (Boulder, Colo.: EDUCAUSE Center for Applied Research, research study, vol. 1, 2004), <http://www.educause.edu/LibraryDetailPage/666?ID=ERS0401>.

8. Brian Hawkins and Deanna Marcum, "Leadership Challenges for the Campus and the Profession," in *Technology Everywhere: A Campus Agenda for Educating and Managing Workers in the Digital Age*, Brian L. Hawkins, Julia A. Rudy, and William H. Wallace, Jr., eds., EDUCAUSE Leadership Strategies, vol. 6 (San Francisco: Jossey-Bass, 2002), pp. 127–137, <http://www.educause.edu/ir/library/pdf/pub7006k.pdf>.

9. Leslie Hitch, Pamela Erskine, and Beth-Anne Dancause, "Filling a Void in IT Professional Development: Understanding Higher Education" (Boulder, Colo.: EDUCAUSE Center for Applied Research, research bulletin, issue 12, 2004), <http://www.educause.edu/LibraryDetailPage/666?ID=ERB0412>.

Acknowledgments

This book is the result of the good thinking, talented writing, and thoughtful review of many people, all of whom have contributed to the rich content of the chapters that follow.

For me it has been a great honor to work with the authors of the chapters in this book, and I would like to thank them for sharing their wisdom and ideas with all of us. All the authors share a common trait—the desire to "give back" to the profession, and they have done so not only through their contributions to this endeavor, but through their own professional activities.

Our information technology community in higher education is filled with people who are committed to helping the next generation of IT professionals grow and develop. Members of the EDUCAUSE Professional Development Committee as well as faculty of the EDUCAUSE Institutes played an important role in the generation of topics and refinement of the prospectus for this book, and they give generously of their time and talent to enhance the contribution that IT makes to higher education.

My colleagues at EDUCAUSE, especially Brian Hawkins and the executive team, Carole Barone, Richard Katz, Mark Luker, and Diana Oblinger, have all contributed to the development of the ideas in this book, and have provided me with support and encouragement in this and all professional development activities.

Finally, I'd like to thank Jeremy, Hannah, and Emma Somers for their love, patience, and encouragement.

—Cynthia Golden
Pittsburgh, Pennsylvania

Part I:
The Organizational
Perspective

CHAPTER 1

Perspectives on IT Leadership

James D. Bruce
MIT

Brian McDonald
MOR Associates, Inc.

At one time IT was the new frontier, and early IT leaders were considered pioneers exploring undiscovered territory. These technically capable, strong individuals brought about breakthroughs in computing few could have imagined during the emergence of IT. As a result, some of them found themselves in leadership positions, wondering exactly how it happened. After all, it was the excitement offered by the new frontier and the potential for making the next great discovery that attracted these inquisitive individuals. As you might imagine, many of them had little knowledge of or interest in management or organizational matters. A pioneer's excitement is piqued by what lies beyond the horizon.

Personal Reflection: Bruce

In the early 1980s, Bill Dickson, then MIT's senior vice president, asked me to talk with him about computing. Some weeks and three conversations later, he asked me to lead MIT's central computing activities: computing services, data center operations, administrative computing, and telephone services. At that time, MIT had no computer network. Its computing environment included some four or five mainframes providing batch and time-sharing services, less than a hundred minicomputers, and no personal computers.

After carefully reflecting on his offer and consulting with colleagues, I told Bill yes. I had previously held senior leadership responsibilities at MIT, and I knew IT reasonably well. That knowledge and skill set, I thought, would be enough. But I now know that when I took the position, I lacked a key set of skills that I will call "leadership competencies."

Being a competent leader requires that you have the skills and knowledge necessary to reach your personal and organizational goals. Assuming that this means primarily technological skills and knowledge, for years we have appointed some of our best technologists to technology leadership positions. But like me some two plus decades ago, most of these people have toolkits that are incomplete. Their tools focus too much on the content of the work—technology, which of course is essential—and far too little on what leaders really do and how they do it.

---◇

IT—the Innovative Frontier

The idea of computing engines dates back at least to Babbage's mechanical difference engine in 1822. Almost a century and a quarter later, in 1946, the first electronic, general-purpose, programmable machine, the ENIAC, was built at the University of Pennsylvania's Moore School of Electrical Engineering. In spite of IBM Chairman Thomas Watson's memorable statement in 1943, "I think there's a world market for maybe five computers," from that date forward the march of computing technology advancements—hardware, system software, and applications—has been exciting and relentless:

▸ 1949—The first stored program computer was built.

▸ 1951—Magnetic core memory entered the picture.

▸ 1953—Transistors replaced vacuum tubes.

▸ 1957—FORTRAN was written.

▸ 1960—Time-sharing made computers more accessible.

▸ 1963—J. C. R. Licklider argued that computers need to speak to each other in a common language.[1]

▸ 1969—ARPANET came into existence with four nodes.

▸ 1971—E-mail, which had been available on stand-alone, time-shared computers, became available between machines on the ARPANET.

▸ 1973—Ethernet invented, becoming the standard technology for local area networks.

▸ 1975—The Altair 8800 personal computer kit brought computers to consumers.

▸ 1981—IBM introduced personal computers.

▸ 1984—Apple created the Macintosh.

▸ 1991—Tim Berners-Lee released the first Web browser to the high-energy physics community at CERN.

▶ 2002—MIT debuted OpenCourseWare with the goal of making almost all of MIT's subjects available on the Web, free of charge, to anyone, anywhere.

This march of advancing technology and applications will continue, driven by human inquisitiveness and by Moore's Law[2] (along with its corollaries focusing on computer memory and network bandwidth). Within a decade we can expect to see computers that are some 100 times more performant and applications that are highly visual, interactive, and collaborative.

A careful look back at this march forward finds many instances where the goal was to achieve a specific technical objective. Leaders, who were experts on the technology and its underlying science and engineering, focused on discovery and development of new technology. They were giants in the new field, like Howard Aiken and Grace Hopper, who designed the MARK series of computers at Harvard in the 1940s; Presper Eckert and John Mauchly, who designed ENIAC at the University of Pennsylvania; Jay Forrester, who invented the magnetic core memory; Fernando Corbató, who was a pioneer in the development of time-sharing; and Jerry Saltzer, who was technical director of Project Athena, one of the first large client-server computing environments. In each of these instances, the true frontier was building the new technology. While these leaders always had a planned application in mind, to a large extent their philosophy was "If we build it, they will come" and "More technology will enable more good things." To a large extent they were correct.

Fast forward to today and look into the future. While many computer scientists and information technologists today are working in their laboratories to push the frontier forward with new IT, new IT systems, and new IT applications, the context has changed. Technology is no longer new and at the periphery of people's lives—including university faculty, staff, and students—but is ubiquitous or very nearly so. The university's central IT mission has shifted from primarily the creation and early use of new technology to its effective and efficient use by everyone. This requires a shift in leadership focus, from creating the technology to making existing and new technology work for clients. Key strengths that were valued in the past are not sufficient for today's IT leaders (see Table 1).

Different Times, Expanded Skill Sets

Similarly, innovation is shifting to the configuration of open, community source, and commercial systems for campus use and to improving support services for a sophisticated client community with expectations driven by experiences with the best commercial software and online options. The territory once occupied by

Table 1. Shifting Leadership

From	To
Technical leader	Capable leader/manager
Subject matter expert	Technically astute and able to facilitate common solutions
Respected resource with the answer	One voice among many
Specialist	Generalist working across organizational units and the university
Technology centric	Strategic thinking from a university view
Narrow expertise	Continuous learner

pioneers and early adopters has attracted many new users who want the technology to facilitate their work. These clients want to do whatever computing they choose, wherever and whenever they choose. Meeting the requirements of the many means providing more stable, seamless, and integrated systems. Providing the various constituents from the faculty to the students and the administrators with this computing experience requires leaders with broader toolkits than those possessed by the early pioneers.

Today, university IT leaders face an increasingly complex environment. Technically, they receive requests for new systems and demands for interoperability, security, and authentication and authorization across trust hierarchies. Nontechnically, they must respond to new and conflicting demands from multiple constituencies and increasing expectations from clients, along with the need to continuously improve operating processes in order to increase client satisfaction, to include decentralized IT groups in the planning process, and to address a multitude of priorities. This complexity calls for leadership that is not only technologically astute but also skilled in competencies more important now than when IT was the new frontier.

IT Leadership and the Required Competencies

At the apex of a leader's responsibility is the strategic challenge involved in determining the right things for the IT group to take on to provide needed services to the university. This is hardly a simple task in complex environments with multiple demands and conflicting interests. Today, senior leaders also know that deciding on the right things to do means setting the ethical standards for the organization as well as the strategic direction.

Once a leadership team decides (in collaboration with others) on the right things to do, the team needs to assess whether the needed talent occupies the roles necessary to accomplish the desired tasks. Significant shifts in strategies or priorities require an analysis of the resources needed to accomplish the desired goals. In the end, most leaders will be judged on their ability to deliver results. After some period of time, senior leaders at the university want to see the progress outlined in the plan. Today's executive IT leaders need to

▶ decide on the right things for the IT group to pursue,

▶ put in place or develop the talent needed to achieve the desired direction, and

▶ deliver the results.

This description of a leader's actions doesn't necessarily reveal the leadership behaviors that allow some people to execute well while others have great difficulty. During the spring and summer of 2004, we conducted an informal survey of CIOs at a group of leading higher education institutions in order to build a list of those competencies needed to fulfill the leadership and management roles particular to university-based IT environments in the coming years. Through these conversations we identified 10 competencies that IT leaders need:

▶ **Strategic thinking from a systems perspective.** The leader contributes to the organization's development of a vision and priorities, anticipates the future, and builds scenarios based on explicit assumptions.

▶ **Shared leadership.** The leader builds working relationships with co-workers and external parties, negotiates and handles problems without alienating people, obtains cooperation through influence, and delegates both responsibility and authority appropriately.

▶ **Communication and persuasion.** The leader distills ideas into focused messages that inspire support or action from others and effectively communicates through presentations, recommendations, or writing. The leader uses appropriate interpersonal styles to guide and persuade individuals and groups.

▶ **Change management.** The leader acts as a catalyst for the needed changes, develops plans, and follows through on change initiatives.

▶ **Decision making.** The leader gathers and uses data and analysis to make decisions, including evaluating the long-term consequences, and makes decisions judged to be right for the university.

▶ **Financial and business acumen.** The leader possesses financial savvy and demonstrates the ability to lead cost-efficient initiatives without sacrificing quality. He or she successfully leads projects and programs that produce favorable results (business and financial outcomes) and demonstrates understanding of the changing financial constructs supporting IT.

▶ **Working across the organization, developing strategic partnerships.** The leader develops networks and alliances, collaborates across boundaries, and finds common ground with a wide range of stakeholders. He or she can maneuver through political situations effectively to get things done.

▶ **Managing complex projects.** The leader maps and manages complex initiatives, continually adjusts plans and strategies based on new information, and identifies and coordinates appropriate resources to support objectives.

▶ **Building agreement.** The leader recognizes different points of view, brings them out into the open, and builds on areas of agreement, exercising influence in ways that enhance the support needed to advance initiatives and building consensus when appropriate.

▶ **Self-knowledge.** The leader knows his or her own personal strengths, weaknesses, opportunities, and limits; seeks feedback; and gains insight from mistakes.

The context and the competencies have changed for leaders taking on responsibility for guiding IT organizations during these increasingly complex times in higher education. These competencies are relevant for more than just IT leaders in executive roles—leadership is needed at many levels within IT. Developing these competencies more broadly will allow many members of the IT community to participate in everyday leadership.

Leadership Roles

IT leaders play various roles inside their organization, inside their university, and in the community at large. These roles could be described as follows:

▶ **Strategist**—builds agreement on the right things, providing a shared strategic direction that, for example, outlines the responsibilities of the central IT organization and how these responsibilities can complement the work of decentralized IT organizations.

▶ **Developer**—designs and delivers increased capabilities (capacity and services), potentially via multiple channels.

▶ **Catalyst**—explores common solutions in order to leverage the knowledge and experience available; makes use of partnerships and consortia.

- **Advocate**—formulates policy, potentially articulating the position of higher education on broader public policy issues.
- **Innovator**—initiates collaborative endeavors, entering into selective partnerships to create what is needed for the future.
- **Ringmaster**—orchestrates a set of coordinated activities, initiating projects, proposing changes where needed, and empowering people to step up and take on the responsibility to bring initiatives to fruition.

What does this mean for IT leaders? Much like the field itself, where often it seems like a sea change is under way, those willing to provide leadership to IT organizations will find themselves in a sea of change. The context, the competencies, the constituencies, the challenges, and the need for more client-centric and collaborative approaches create a confluence that shifts the very landscape for IT leaders.

The pioneers made tremendous contributions to advancing IT, and untold innovations are yet to come. Still, the landscape has changed, and there is a graying of long-term IT leaders in higher education. This makes it incumbent on those of us turning over the reins to support the development of competencies needed by those stepping up to lead mature, complex organizations. One of the most important jobs any leader has is to develop the next generation of leaders.

There are many ways to enhance leadership development within IT organizations:

- Make sure the hiring requirements reflect the need for technical competency and the broader skill sets related to leadership so that those entering employment opportunities in higher education arrive with the necessary prerequisites. It may also be useful to create a developmental ladder for new hires so that they can see the skill sets they are expected to develop.
- Provide the experiences and exposure that enable people to expand their horizons and capabilities. In a recent set of informal interviews we conducted, when asked what helped them learn about leadership, participants repeatedly mentioned on-the-job opportunities. Individuals found stretch assignments to be one of the most important contributors to their growth. In addition, they mentioned how attending meetings at a higher level or being put on a cross-functional team hastened their development.[3] Creating opportunities for individuals to work within other divisions in IT can expand their knowledge and break down organizational barriers.

▸ Take a more deliberative approach to fostering distributive leadership in IT. Leadership need not be restricted to a few senior directors or the CIO. It will help to cultivate leadership competencies at multiple levels in IT. There are hundreds of interactions between IT staff and clients throughout the university. If the knowledge workers in IT can become more strategic, communicate better with clients, help build agreements with clients, and become catalysts for needed changes, then the executives' job will be to foster these constructive behaviors.

▸ IT organizations need to create career ladders that provide technical leaders an alternative pathway to exercising influence. A core competency in any IT organization will continue to be technical proficiency, and some technologists may not have an interest in or aptitude for the broader leadership skills outlined here.

▸ Be more explicit about helping IT managers develop their leadership capabilities. Investing in the development of staff will provide your organization with a favorable return. Finding a formula for integrating development into the way people learn while they work will help them to continue to grow and evolve in a field that demands people keep up or be left behind. Stretch assignments, mentoring, action learning, and other approaches are simply a means to this end.

Conclusion

The context for IT has changed during the past few decades. The stakes are higher now that IT has come of age. There are still new frontiers to explore, but IT has become a mainstream service. Innovation needs to be done in protected arenas to shield people from the disruptions that marked the IT landscape in the early days. University leaders expect IT to deliver the seamless services required by those who find this technology integral to their work. IT must compete with other university organizations and priorities for the funding that once was handed to the pioneers who made bold predictions about this promising field.

IT leaders must evolve as the higher education IT environment continues to change. The next generation will need to develop new competencies and adapt as the landscape shifts. As pioneers settled into any new frontier, it became essential to bring order to chaos, to create organization and authority. Those joining the pioneers wanted to feel secure, to be assured of reliable services before they would embrace these new territories. The clients IT serves want much the same, and that requires leaders capable of delivering technology and much more. Being a continuous learner may well be the best way to prepare for the uncertain future ahead.

Personal Reflection: Bruce

Over my many years in IT, I came to believe it was important for me as a leader to reflect on three aspects of my leadership: be, do, learn.

Be—*To be an effective leader you must have character. Followers want leaders who have character. Who are you? What are your values? People want leaders who are credible.*

Do—*I have come to believe the leader's work most often focuses on two fundamental sets of tasks: coping with organizational complexity, and coping with change. Both involve deciding what needs to be done, developing the capacity to get it done, and ensuring that it is done. The leader must be deeply involved at all levels in the doing that will achieve the vision, whether by providing resources, removing obstacles, monitoring results, or doing whatever is required.*

Learn—*To lead effectively, you must face each day as an active learner. Max De Pree wrote, "The rate of change requires that each of us become a frantic learner. Leaders respond to change by learning something new."*[4]

These three touchstones have served me well. I hope you adopt touchstones that can provide you solid footing in a constantly changing IT world.

Endnotes

1. A number of Licklider's writings as well as writings about him point to his making a case for standards among computers. For more on his work, see <http://www.ibiblio.org/pioneers/licklider.html>.

2. Empirical observation attributed to Gordon E. Moore, cofounder of Intel, that the complexity of an integrated circuit will double every 18 months. With an increase in complexity, size and cost for a given functionality decrease. See <http://en.wikipedia.org/wiki/Moore's_law>.

3. These observations are supported by earlier work done at the Center for Creative Leadership and published by Morgan W. McCall, Ann M. Morrison, and Michael M. Lombardo in *The Lessons of Experience: How Successful Executives Develop on the Job* (Lanham, Md.: Lexington Books, 1988).

4. Max De Pree, *Leadership Jazz* (New York: Currency DoubleDay, 1992), p. 84.

About the Authors

James D. Bruce is a professor emeritus of electrical engineering and vice president emeritus for information systems at the Massachusetts Institute of Technology in Cambridge. He was responsible for MIT's central information technology environment from 1983 to 2003. Bruce received bachelor's degrees in electrical engineering and in mathematics from the Lamar State College of Technology in Beaumont, Texas, and his master's and doctorate from the Massachusetts Institute of Technology.

Brian McDonald is president of MOR—Maximizing Organizational Resources—Associates, Inc., created in 1983 to assist clients in developing strategies designed to elicit the contributions employees want to make to enhance the success of their enterprise. He has increasingly focused on developing leaders, enhancing strategic thinking, and consulting on continuous improvement efforts. McDonald received his undergraduate degree from the University of Massachusetts and his master's from Boston University. Bruce and he currently present the Information Technology Leaders Program to IT managers from U.S. research universities.

CHAPTER 2

A Comprehensive Approach to Professional Development for an IT Staff

Gene Spencer and Jeannie Zappe
Bucknell University

Take a moment to reflect on the experience of your organization over the past decade as it supported the mission of your institution. It should be fairly easy to recognize key moments of dramatic change driven by clearly identifiable major events or longer periods of persistent changes (as minor as they may have seemed at the time) that proved a catalyst for significant organizational trial and transformation. Consider how those events and conditions shaped the future of your organization and its ability to succeed over time.

Change can occur for any number of reasons, including the arrival or departure of a key institutional leader, increased interest in a particular issue by a governing board, a significant new advance in technology, a new institutional strategic plan, or a groundswell of demand from a key stakeholder group. Other catalysts might be more subtle but no less transformative for an IT organization's focus and operation over the long term—a newly elected chair of a faculty advisory committee, a key vendor's withdrawal from the market, a budget shortfall, a major grant or gift, or the arrival or departure of a key member of the IT staff.

Change can happen at any time. We can't predict which events and conditions will be the most transformative until the passage of time brings clarity and perspective. How, then, can we create the climate and conditions for success for our staff, our organization, and ourselves in the face of a rapidly changing environment that we cannot possibly control?

At Bucknell University, we identified several key events and changes in the environment that contributed significantly to moments of change for the IT organization. Our catalysts included the end of the mainframe era (which also signaled the end of our ability to effectively build our own administrative applications), the creation of a new faculty computing advisory committee (with a focused vision for how technology might enhance the curriculum), the retirement of a long-standing director of the library (ending a productive chapter in the library's development and opening the door to new organizational options), and the arrival of new campus leaders willing to take the risk of merging the library and IT organizations as an investment in the institution's future.

In our earliest moments of dealing with these complex transitions, we identified the lack of a firm and cohesive commitment to professional development (PD) within the IT staff and a lack of ongoing organizational development of the IT organization as some of our greatest obstacles to success. The challenges we faced required a level of flexibility and adaptability in our organization that we had not previously achieved. New technologies and ways of working with our colleagues and with the campus community required an enhanced set of skills that could allow our organization to succeed in the midst of overwhelming change. We needed to prepare our staff colleagues for unanticipated and complex situations by helping build technical skills and cultivate individual attributes such as agility, curiosity, service orientation, empowerment, collaboration, self-motivation, leadership, accountability, and a willingness to embrace change and take appropriate risks. With these characteristics and skills, people could increasingly find themselves in a position where they could succeed, thus creating an environment of positive morale and providing a foundation for dealing with the next season of change or wave of transformation. Professional and organizational development became key components of our ongoing organizational change strategy.

Conversation, Commitment, and Concerted Effort

Far too often, IT organizations find themselves without the necessary resources and tools to develop their staffs in effective ways. Budgets for training and development are sorely lacking and often the first thing sacrificed when difficult choices must be made. Individual staff are often too busy to learn necessary skills—ironically, they are "too busy sawing wood to stop and sharpen the saw." The most common tools for learning tend to be trial-and-error or learn-by-doing. These approaches work well for some individuals in some instances, but prove too slow or ineffective in others. In too many cases, attempts are made to solve problems without the benefit of the most appropriate tools because individuals simply do not have the latest skills to apply.

What would it take to change this picture? What kinds of resources would be necessary for the IT organization to foster an appropriate culture of learning within its staff? Fortunately, there is no single right way to apply professional development to an organization. Virtually any investment in PD can provide some positive benefit or momentum, and progress can be made in small, incremental steps if it is reasonably focused and if it engages the right individuals appropriately.

In our transformation at Bucknell, three key elements provided a foundation for sustained progress: conversation, commitment, and concerted effort.

As we started the first significant change process, we engaged in a series of conversations about the need for increased PD. We initiated a discourse within the organization and with the leadership of the institution; we spoke at length with anyone who would listen about our case for improved PD, citing the need for better service, better troubleshooting skills, quicker response, and improved solutions. We talked about the skills we needed to develop, while acknowledging that investing in those skills might make our staff more attractive to the external job market. (We firmly believed that creating an organization where people could learn and grow would encourage them to stay, and we were proven right.) We explained openly what support people would need and gave them that support. Most importantly, we created an environment where our staff could direct their own development efforts in ways that made sense to them, rather than having PD "done to them."

Next, our organization made a conscious commitment to increase the priority given to training and development. As a first step, we put more of our financial resources into the budget for PD activities. We looked for ways to build the necessary training into every major project we undertook. (As with most colleges and universities, it was much easier to get funding for projects, systems, and networks than it was to get approval to hire extra staff or provide adequate training.) With the proper emphasis and justification, we were able to initially double the funds annually set aside for training activities because the argument simply made a great deal of sense: at a time when the campus community wanted our services to improve, we argued that training and staff development were key elements of the solution.

These conversations and commitments have become a habitual part of our organizational culture. They started modestly and grew from year to year, representing a concerted effort within our organization. We talk regularly about the ongoing development of the organization as the environment changes around us. Issues of professional development now pervade our discussions during the hiring process and in our conversations with new staff members, engaging them in a commitment to take responsibility for helping define their own PD needs. We have built self-assessment, feedback from colleagues, and goal-setting into our annual performance planning process so that it focuses more on the future than on shortcomings of the past. We have set an expectation that individuals are responsible for identifying and addressing their own PD activities, given the appropriate coaching and resources to do so. Most importantly, we have a strong commitment to protect (and even overspend) the funds set aside for PD, even during years when we need to aggressively trim budgets.

Finally, a key characteristic of this concerted effort is the ongoing assessment of our environment. At times, we approach professional and organizational development activities passionately and aggressively because of a perceived need and openness within the organization. At other times, we take a measured and subtle approach, sensing that the moment is not yet right and the opportunity needs to develop. Just as there are cycles of change, there are cycles in the developmental process that should not be ignored.

A Complex Interrelationship

The needs of the individual, the organization, and the institution are inextricably connected. Recognizing the complexity and dynamic nature of this interrelationship is an important component of success. IT professionals can easily be motivated to engage in those developmental activities that most closely meet the needs of their primary technical responsibilities. Other development activities, however, might actually provide a larger benefit for the organization or the institution as a whole, a benefit that an individual might not fully appreciate. For example, the IT organization may sorely need to engage in team-building skills or other collaborative skills such as coaching or problem resolution, yet these activities might seem like a lower priority to someone with a major project deadline bearing down.

At Bucknell, we engage in a regular discourse about the varying needs of the institution and the needs of the IT organization, to help colleagues understand the broader context. For example, we have invited key members of the university administration to talk to our staff about their roles in the mission of the university and how our organization supports them. We regularly engage in a state-of-the-university discussion at our departmental staff meetings. Our leadership team regularly sends "making connections" messages to all of our staff in an effort to create context, make connections between seemingly random events, and help continuously mold organizational culture.

The 1997 merger of IT and the library at Bucknell provided our new organization with an excellent opportunity to focus on organizational development. In blending two staffs comprised of 90 individuals from two very different (and seemingly incompatible) organizational cultures, we felt an obvious need to create some consistency in vision, values, and organizational culture for the new organization.[1] Our chief information officer at the time took two masterful approaches: he engaged two organizational development consultants to help us in our organizational work, and he defined a principle for moving forward called *opportunistic evolution*—to look for opportunities when people were ready to move forward and seize them in an evolutionary, nonthreatening way.

From our resulting organizational development work emerged a shared statement of vision and values for the new Department of Information Services and Resources (ISR).[2] While this statement has undergone two significant revisions in intervening years, the values remain true to the organization we were attempting to create from the start. See Figure 1 for the current version of those values.

Figure 1. Bucknell University Information Services and
Resources Values Statement

Our Values Statement: Within Information Services and Resources, we share a common set of values as we work to accomplish our mission of supporting the academic, administrative, and co-curricular functions of Bucknell University. These values provide us with a framework for effectively working together and meeting the needs of the campus community. They are ideals toward which we continue to strive in our daily efforts.

1. We value our role in the mission of the university.
2. We value exceptional customer service.
3. We value a collaborative work environment.
4. We value leadership throughout the organization.
5. We value professional expertise and professional development.
6. We value personal accountability.
7. We value a healthy work environment.
8. We refuse to let each other fail.

Our staff understand what these values represent, and they have been a powerful force in creating an environment where we can succeed together. Obviously, the first two values speak to our commitment to the institution and what it needs from us in terms of alignment, service, and skills. Our technical skills are irrelevant if not fully aligned with institutional needs or if we do not serve the community effectively. The third and fourth values define how we will work together as an organization, how we will relate to one another, and what expectations we can have about our joint work. The fifth and sixth values declare the attributes we require from one another, which include a focus on and responsibility for PD (in all of its forms). The final two values are simply commitments we make to each other about the ways we work in healthy and mutually supportive ways.

Over the years, our organization has worked to further explore and describe what each of these values means to each of us. At the same time, we have continued to reinvent ourselves in ways that are appropriate to our changing environment and to build an environment where we can all succeed together. More importantly, embedded within these values are several commitments that have allowed us to focus on the full range of developmental activities for the organization, such as professional skills, collaborative skills, and leadership skills.

Professional, Collaborative, and Leadership Skills

Professional development can have a wide range of meanings and can be accomplished in various ways. Many people in IT organizations, however, will focus primarily on the technical skills most useful within the technologies their work involves.[3] These tend to be skills related to particular software and hardware systems, troubleshooting approaches, tool sets, security initiatives, and other elements of IT technologies. People can be more easily motivated in these areas because such skills often represent the interests and passions that originally attracted them to a job in our organization in the first place.

The other major component of PD activities falls into a category commonly referred to as soft skills or people skills. Unfortunately, IT professionals too often view these terms in a pejorative sense as being less important than the technical skills that enable them to do their work.

At Bucknell, our statement of values helps create a vocabulary for effectively discussing this sensitive issue. Naming our culture ("our collaborative work environment") has allowed us to subsume a variety of developmental activities often seen as soft skills under an umbrella we refer to as *collaborative skills*. As technologies have become increasingly interrelated and integrated, most IT professionals can easily see the value of collaboration in accomplishing their work. Thus, they are likely to be more open to gaining the collaborative skills that help us work effectively together (including working with the external community).

Creating an expectation of leadership throughout the organization also creates an opportunity to engage the staff in another set of important skills, centered on the need for all of us to display leadership characteristics and behaviors. These skills are often considered the responsibility of a few people in a leadership position (the typical notion of leadership as a hierarchy). We consider the broad definition of leadership as "the skill of influencing people to work enthusiastically toward goals identified as being for the common good."[4] Clearly, we have people in defined leadership positions, but we also set out to build an overall climate where any individual can posses and exhibit the skills and behaviors required to take on a leadership role in an area appropriate to his or her abilities, interests, and span of influence. In fact, our collaborative work environment coupled with our relatively flat organization depends heavily on the sharing of leadership throughout the entire staff rather than relying on the relatively few individuals designated as managers.

Our statement of jointly held values provides a significant benefit for us in creating an environment in which the skills we need to develop organizationally can be viewed as equal components of a larger, more comprehensive professional development program embracing both technical skills and soft skills.

Engaging the Right People

The challenge of creating and sustaining a comprehensive approach to PD seems enormous at the outset, and the perceived obstacles can easily get in the way of even beginning to make such a commitment. Thinking about what it might take to build and maintain momentum might deter mere mortals. The solution to overcoming this obstacle is simple: make modest plans, be persistent, and engage enough of the right people in the process.

Over the course of several years and multiple transitions, ISR at Bucknell has taken many approaches to the development of our staff and organization. At one point, we appointed a single development leader to get a program started and provided a few thousand dollars for team training. Later, the leadership team took on the task and broadened the effort. Still later, we appointed a

Staff Development Team comprised of individuals from across the organization. Each of these approaches had some success within the environment at the time; each was replaced by the next iteration because its season had passed. We expected progress rather than perfection from these programs.

Our current Organizational Development Team (ODT) has been our greatest asset in the ongoing development of ISR. This group represents individuals from across the organization (most of whom do not hold leadership or managerial roles) and is led by a staff member who is deeply committed to our values and development goals. The group engages the talents and energies of people who are keenly interested in and passionate about PD and the growth of our organization. Each year, some members of the team step down and others are invited to join; most are self-motivated and ask to be a part of this work, so the group has a built-in process of self-renewal.

The energy within this group is astounding. One challenge has been to ensure that the team's work aligns well with the activities of the entire organization. In particular, special care must be taken to define our major developmental activities in concert with the ebb and flow of the organization's workflow. For example, it is critical for us to limit the major activities of ODT so they don't occur during the busy summer installation season, even though some members of the team find more slack time then. The keys to this alignment are simple: one member of our leadership team sits on ODT as a full member, and our department head regularly joins the team meetings. In addition, the team meets as a whole with ISR's leadership team on a regular basis to engage in a conversation about priorities over the next several months.

Having a team or group with the responsibility of continually focusing on professional and organizational development has been critical to our success. Further, the work becomes more manageable when shared among team members. ODT's charge has changed and evolved with the organization. In the beginning, they focused on the basic skills required to succeed in our collaborative work environment: giving and receiving feedback, coaching, communication skills and strategies, good meeting skills, celebrating the successes of our collaborative work environment, and Myers-Briggs Type Indicator (MBTI) training. Their work has also focused on activities that keep our organizational values alive and celebrated. For example, we focused on one value per month for an entire year by hosting one or more related development opportunities.

ODT's current purpose and mission (which will guide their work and activities for the next several years) follow:

> ODT's purpose is to serve as a partner to ISR's leadership team in being stewards of a healthy organization that best serves the needs of the university. Together, we will set a learning agenda that the organization needs over the next 3–5 years. ODT will then focus directly on the implementation of that learning agenda. ODT should also help ISR keep its focus on: our values, our collaborative work environment, our alignment with Bucknell's core competencies, improving our technical and professional skills, improving our organizational and collaboration skills, and shaping our new employee orientation program.

Additional Examples of Bucknell Efforts

In addition to the activities mentioned above, the ODT (in partnership with our leadership team) has hosted or sponsored varied professional and organizational development activities and initiatives over the past several years. A list of our most successful strategies follows:

▶ We retained the services of an outside organizational development consultant who we use in the early phases of training initiatives and change processes, or when an activity might best be facilitated by someone from outside our organization.

▶ We partner regularly with members of our human resources staff in areas where their skills and resources can best help.

▶ We have a weekly staff meeting called Thursdays@10, where any staff member can share information with our entire staff, teach a new skill, or facilitate a discussion. Attendance is optional and based on individual preferences and availability, but roughly 50 percent of our staff attend any particular session.

▶ We created two Staff Development Centers, which our staff can use for PD activities or as quiet space for reading, projects, or self-paced learning. Both centers also contain libraries of our favorite books and resources, including some of the latest books on leadership, staff recognition, managing change, personal accountability, and much more.

▶ We foster an environment of reading and learning about new ideas in the areas that we believe will help our organization. Our leadership team regularly shares books with each other and staff.

- Within ISR, the largest portion of our PD budget goes to the development of technical skills. We understand and accept that these conferences and technical training activities are expensive and worthwhile.
- We also create an environment where staff members regularly share those skills with each other.
- A significant percentage of visible PD activities for our staff are devoted to collaborative skills and leadership skills.
- Training sessions have been provided on many key areas, such as giving and receiving feedback, coaching, communication skills and strategies, good meeting skills, and the MBTI training.
- We encourage members of our staff to get involved in professional organizations (such as EDUCAUSE) in a serious way, serving on boards, planning committees and task committees, and making presentations and teaching.
- We focus regularly on living our values. For example, we held an exercise to tell stories throughout the entire ISR staff about successful collaborations that occur because of our collaborative work environment.
- We took 14 members of our staff to an appreciative inquiry conference and have let that knowledge and information slowly permeate our organization.
- We find exceptional developmental activities such as the EDUCAUSE Management Institute and regularly send one or two individuals to each session.
- We created an ISR intranet that includes materials from previous PD activities, organizational skill development resources, and a list of professional organizations.
- Our leadership team all have the following in their job descriptions: "To be successful, you must have a passion for your own professional development that includes developing leadership qualities in yourself and others."
- We specifically focus on issues of PD in the hiring process to identify needs, as well as to recruit the most desirable candidates.

Conclusion

We believe that the case can easily be made for a comprehensive approach to PD that can help an IT staff operate at its best. While there is no single right way to approach such a venture, the attention given to both individuals and the staff as a whole can pay ongoing dividends to the entire organization as it becomes better able to face the array of challenges that the future will bring. Clearly there are benefits to improving individual technical skills. But more importantly, an organization can become a more cohesive unit by developing skills and competencies for effectively working together. We have found that creating shared meaning, building a vocabulary for discourse, and enabling better organizational understanding have contributed to creating an empowered and agile staff who continually leverage our collaborative work environment. Further, we feel ready for the next changes that we will face because our staff knows and values our commitment to doing whatever is needed in terms of professional development and preparedness.

Endnotes

1. This work can easily occur without the trauma of a drastic organizational event such as the merger of two departments. In this case, the merger simply created an awareness of the need and a willingness to act that might not have occurred otherwise.

2. To learn more about Information Services and Resources at Bucknell University, please visit <http://www.bucknell.edu/isr/>, in particular the "About ISR" section of the Web site.

3. We use the term *technologies* in the broadest possible sense here.

4. James C. Hunter, *The Servant: A Simple Story About the True Essence of Leadership* (Roseville, Calif.: Prima Publishing, 1998).

About the Authors

Gene Spencer is the associate vice president for information services and resources at Bucknell University. He serves an integrated library/IT organization with responsibility for all aspects of computing services, library services, networking, instructional technology, enterprise information systems, library collections, information access, and telecommunications. He focuses primarily on organizational development, leadership development, and creating a collaborative work environment. Spencer currently is the director of the EDUCAUSE Management Institute and serves on the EDUCAUSE Professional Development Committee and the InCommon Federation Steering Committee. He is active in the Consortium of Liberal Arts Colleges (CLAC) and the Oberlin Group of Library Directors.

Jeannie Zappe is the director of service integration in information services and resources at Bucknell University, where she leads the technology support group, serves on the organization's leadership team, and plays a leading role in ongoing organizational development and service focus in the merged IT/library environment. She also manages the centralized functions of the department's contingent of student employees. She has worked in various IT roles at Bucknell, including user support, training, hiring, and staff development. She served on the EDUCAUSE Professional Development Committee and from 1998 to 2003 on the faculty of the EDUCAUSE Institute Management Program.

CHAPTER 3

Organizational Strategies for Fostering a Culture of Learning

Marilu Goodyear, Kathleen Ames-Oliver, and Keith Russell
University of Kansas

A Vision of Organizational Learning

When we think of leadership within information services organizations, we often focus on the technology: implementing it and managing it. Since it is logical to assume that getting the work done is our ultimate goal, a focus on the tasks of work makes sense to us. The constant activity of our daily lives reinforces the view that getting the work done should be our focus. However, if we truly understand what the work is about, we immediately understand that most "work" is accomplished through people. It is the dedication, motivation, knowledge, and skill sets of individuals that make a tremendous difference in the organization. Marcus Buckingham pointed out in his keynote speech at the EDUCAUSE Annual Conference in 2004 that the American Management Association's motto "Getting Work Done Through People" is exactly backwards—our goal really is to "Get People Done Through Work."[1]

Our professional literature leads us to consider the infrastructures needed within an information services organization for us to be effective. It is common to discuss the organizational infrastructure in the sense of how to organize the work and the technical infrastructure in relation to the technology used. As IT organizations have matured, the focus on the service infrastructure of the organization has increased, including its link to user services, project management, and process improvement[2] through such programs as Information Technology Infrastructure Library (ITIL). Our purpose here is to outline a fourth infrastructure to join organizational, technical, and service as a focus of leadership attention: the organizational learning infrastructure. Research reported in the professional literature of management, psychology, and other disciplines strongly supports the effectiveness of programs that focus on the development of the employee's collaborative skill set.[3] This research as applied to information services organizations has potential to improve effectiveness.[4] The previous chapter outlined the importance of programs to enhance professional development in these areas. In this chapter, we explain actions by one university to improve IT staff education on our underlying values and the use of facilitation within an information services organization.

The concept of organizational development (OD) is often used to represent the ability of an organization to continuously improve. French and Bell provided an academic and comprehensive definition of OD as "a long-term effort, led and supported by top management, to improve an organization's visioning, empowerment, learning, and problem-solving processes, through an ongoing, collaborative management of organization culture...using the consultant/facilitator role and the theory and technology of applied behavioral science...."[5] On a day-to-day level, a shorthand definition of OD is "an ongoing, thoughtfully planned effort by all members of an organization to improve how that organization operates, serves its stakeholders, fulfills its mission, and approaches its vision."[6]

OD is a discipline built on both academic research and real-world practice in the applications of research findings, all focused on improving the effectiveness of individuals, groups, and organizations. It encompasses a wide range of topics, including organizational behavior, group dynamics, facilitation, continuous improvement, learning organizations, organizational learning, and appreciative inquiry. Many universities recognize the value of OD and are institutionalizing such practices. The National Consortium for Continuous Improvement in Higher Education (NCCI) has more than 60 member institutions focused on the use of continuous improvement (http://www.ncci-cu.org/). A recent work in the library literature focuses on the expanding use of OD in university libraries.[7]

Elements of an Organizational Learning Infrastructure

This chapter outlines the experience of Information Services at the University of Kansas (KU), which includes IT units and libraries, in building an organizational learning infrastructure as a basis for continuous organizational development. Many organizations have adopted organizational effectiveness efforts (for example, team management, facilitation, workflow improvement) without completely realizing the OD research foundation underlying these activities. At KU, we set out to develop a permanent infrastructure, based on the research and literature in this area, focused on the need to develop individual and collective learning skill sets. Organizational learning, as we have used it, is defined as enhancing the capability for learning within the organization.[8] In its current form, the organizational learning infrastructure includes the following elements: the incorporation of values into leadership development, the development of facilitation and other OD capacities, and the development of a mentoring capacity. Our discussion includes these elements as well as the creation of the Organizational Development Group, which enabled Information Services at KU to maintain focus on these issues.

Leadership for Organizational Development

To advance organizational learning, Information Services established an OD community of practice in 2001. Thirteen interested administrators, faculty, and staff from throughout Information Services units and from the KU Department of Human Resources Professional Development unit (KUHRPD, the official campus-wide OD unit) met to discuss the possible formation of such a group and its purpose(s). After exploration, Information Services leadership and the group decided on a dual purpose: to create and nurture a group of facilitators for use within Information Services and KU, and to explore and build capacity for understanding and applying OD concepts, practices, and tools within Information Services and KU. The group became known as the Information Services Organizational Development Group (OD Group).

Now more than four years old, the OD Group has grown to approximately 30 members. It meets several times a year in facilitated discussions led by volunteers from the group or with expert outside presenters. Some of the subjects explored by the group include:

▶ Facilitation
▶ Use of 360° feedback
▶ Generational differences in the workplace
▶ Models for managing change
▶ How to create a culture of assessment
▶ Appreciative inquiry
▶ Time and project management
▶ Organizational values (and how to elicit and use them)
▶ Positive psychology in the workplace

Members of the group regularly share information on OD activities from professional organizations and other campus units. The group sometimes serves as a sounding board for the vice provost for information services as organizational change challenges arise (such as budget reductions).

The OD Group has facilitated bringing the practice of organizational learning into the operations of the units. The group strives to provide expertise and consultation to the organization's leaders and managers. The goal is for leaders to ensure that Information Services has an effective environment for organizational learning and that each employee has the opportunity to develop his or her skills and to apply them in the collaborative work of the organization. As Information Services moves forward with building the organizational learning infrastructure, the OD Group will continue to play an important role in assisting the operational managers in ensuring effective group practice.

Values: A Critical Part of Leadership Development

A critical element in building organizational learning capacity is the development of division and departmental leaders and key managers. At KU, Information Services has 32 individuals who comprise the leadership group. This group includes individuals who hold leadership positions down to the assistant director level and other staff who play important leadership support roles (for example, human resources, budget, and external relations managers). The leadership group meets once a month to focus on issues important for the organization as a whole.

Leadership development is a critical component of building an organizational learning infrastructure, since these individuals ultimately ensure that a capacity to learn is developed and nurtured among staff. Joint understanding of the organizational values that form the basis of a learning environment was seen as the first step. Information Services therefore made the development of values a key component of the strategic planning process. The work started in groups focusing on values as behaviors in action. Facilitators helped the work groups identify the behaviors important to them within the work environment. The results of those discussions were collected into a document and discussed with the leadership group and volunteer representatives from the units. Ultimately, these volunteers and OD Group members brought the full measure of their ideas to the written description of the organization's values. A critical piece in the presentation of the values was linking them to the university and Information Services mission statements (Figure 1) and providing specific links to behaviors that represented our values (Figure 2).

Figure 1. Relationship Between Mission Statements

The University of Kansas Mission
as a major comprehensive research and teaching university, is to serve as a center for learning, scholarship, and creative endeavor.

Our Information Services Mission
is to collaborate with scholars, learners, leaders, managers, and each other to facilitate access to information and the innovative use of technology in support of learning, scholarship, and creative endeavor.

Our Values Support Our Mission

Support for Scholarly Work and Learning	Innovative Applications of Technology
We support the academic community by providing access to information and knowledge.	We provide creative leadership in planning, discovering, and implementing appropriate technologies to support teaching, research, and service.
We are effective stewards of information resources and collections, ensuring accessibility for future generations of scholars.	We focus on what will create excellence, rather than simply what is new or different.
We provide instruction on information-seeking skills and technology use.	

Quality Service	Organizational Learning
We strive to understand, meet, and foresee the needs of our clients and colleagues.	We strive to create a work environment that supports and facilitates growth and learning at the personal, team, and community levels.
We provide high-quality programs and services, and continually seek client feedback and ways to improve.	In this way, we are better able to serve our clients, plan and manage change, and grow together as a service organization.
We seek to exceed expectations whenever possible.	

Valuing the Person and the Professional	Integrity and Growth
We foster an environment where both professional projects and personal endeavors are valued and balanced in a thoughtful and caring way.	We communicate openly and honestly with clients and colleagues; promote respect; embrace change; encourage professional growth; empower one another to take risks; and seek excellence from ourselves and each other.
We celebrate the unique qualities, talents, and commitments that each individual brings to our organization.	

Figure 2. Examples of Behaviors That Represent Values

Realizing the Information Services Vision: What it takes...

Our Clients

Meet their needs (through services)
- *Quality/process focus*
- *Communication*

Foresee their needs (through research and development)
- *Innovation*

Continuously improve/evaluate our services
- *Two-way communication*

Our Selves

- Exhibit *adaptability* to rapid change, shifting priorities
- Take the *initiative*
- Demonstrate *integrity*
- Promote *respect*
- Celebrate *diversity*
- Maximize *productivity*
- Maintain *personal/ professional balance*
- Grow *professionally*
- Be *excellent* at what we do

Our University Community

Maintain *strategic vision* by
- monitoring changing needs within the KU environment
- maintaining awareness of Kansas initiatives and needs
- observing national best practices
- keeping an eye on the big picture
- conducting peer assessments and environmental scans

Seek ways to contribute time, talent, and resources

Our Teams

Use great *management* skills
- *Decision-making and problem solving*
- *Delegation/follow-up*
- *Planning, organizing, implementing*

Employ great *leadership* ability
- Maintain *action orientation*
- Focus on *employee development*
- *Empower* others to take risks
- *Strive* to meet clients' needs and expectations
- Make *interpersonal* relationships a priority
- Maintain *strategic* vision

Communicate clearly and effectively
- Give, solicit, and receive *constructive feedback*
- *Coach* and *be coached*

Promote *teamwork*
- Be a *highly effective* team member
- Address and *manage group conflict*
- *Learn* as a team
- Develop *cross-team cooperation*
- Seek creative ways to *make work fun*

With the values established, Information Services launched an educational program to provide focused experience with what they meant to the leadership group. Given that we could not focus on everything at once, the OD Group and the leadership group discussed the areas most in need of development. Senior leaders also identified the most common elements within the organization that limited our effectiveness. Coordinated by the vice provost for information services, four areas were chosen for attention: improving meeting effectiveness, encouraging risk taking, moving past whining (which became known as Whine Stoppers), and understanding models for implementing organizational change. The consensus of leaders, managers, and staff involved in developing this list was that if the organization could make progress in these four areas, increased organizational effectiveness would follow.

After identification of these topics, teams from the OD Group, assisted by experts from KUHRPD and appropriate university faculty members, developed curricula and presented educational programs in the regular leadership meetings. Table 1 outlines the values, areas chosen for improvement, and curriculum content.

In addition to focusing on values, leaders were asked to develop individual skill sets that would enable them to lead within our collaborative organization. The programs in facilitation and mentoring provided opportunities for these individuals to improve their skill sets.

Facilitation as a Critical Component of Organizational Learning

Collaboration is increasingly important in information services organizations. Ensuring the effectiveness of collaborative processes is a major factor in successful operations and employee productivity.[9] Process facilitators, who are knowledgeable in the stages of group development and experienced in managing group dynamics, can offer a wide array of tools and processes to maximize group effectiveness and efficiency.[10] The word *facilitate* means "to make easy." With every collaborative group, the leader needs to assist the group in two ways: task and process. The facilitator guides the process, thus freeing the group to focus on the task. Most group leaders have task knowledge, so generally do not need much assistance in that area. However, many group leaders would like assistance in organizing meeting processes, building good group cohesion, and using tools for decision making and other purposes. Facilitators can advise the group leader on such matters and assist during collaborative processes. Facilita-

Table 1. Educational Programs Developed to Address Four Key Values Areas

Value	Topic	Elements of the Curriculum
Organizational Learning	Meeting Management	▶ Tips for improving meetings: agendas; roles; using the parking lot not to get sidetracked; establishing ground rules; engaging in return-on-time-invested analysis ▶ Key activities for meeting planners: plan objectives; inform participants; structure and facilitate discussions—control and summarize; record actions and next steps
Organizational Learning	The Change Process	▶ Change is a transition process ▶ People respond differently to change ▶ Change includes loss ▶ What do people feel during the transition? ▶ Gaining commitment to the new reality ▶ Role of managers ▶ The grieving cycle ▶ Meaning and its role in the past and moving forward
Valuing the Person and the Professional	Whine Stoppers	▶ Definitions of whining versus productive criticism ▶ Why do people whine? ▶ Effects on the group ▶ How to move whiners to action/problem solving
Integrity and Growth	Risk Taking	▶ Risk taking defined as goal-oriented creative behavior when the outcome is unclear ▶ Examples of individuals and group risk-taking behavior; table of risk-taking skills; background readings; suggested group practices

tion is more an art than a science. Facilitation skills can be taught, but deciding when and how to employ certain group interventions requires a keen sense of timing and sensitivity on the part of the facilitator. Such abilities seem innate to those who make good facilitators.

Given that we did not have the resources to use external expertise, we chose to develop our own staff as facilitators. The facilitation program includes 11 employees who regularly work in one unit but also facilitate for other Information Services units. Volunteer facilitators were evaluated against the following set of skills as basic prequalifiers:

▶ **Empathic listening**—the ability to listen to individuals and a group at a variety of levels and respond with sensitivity

▶ **Process focus**—the ability to focus only on the process of the group and suppress personal desires for a particular outcome

▶ **Personal organization**—the ability to organize and manage one's personal time and space for maximum efficiency and effectiveness

▶ **Conceptual framework**—the ability to capture a variety of complex ideas at the core of a discussion and synthesize them for the group

▶ **Flexibility**—the ability to change plans and move in an unforeseen direction when the situation demands

▶ **Collaborative learning**—the ability to work with others cooperatively, sharing resources and knowledge

▶ **Sense of timing**—the ability to know when to broach certain topics and when to intervene in potentially sensitive situations

A training program was developed and implemented in collaboration with KUHRPD and two staff members from Information Services. The trainers, experienced in both training and facilitation, developed a program combining conceptual as well as hands-on opportunities for learning in which participants practiced using the tools and processes employed in facilitation. The two-day facilitator training covered the following topics:

▶ Introducing the history, philosophy, and practice of facilitation

▶ Reviewing the role of the facilitator

▶ Outlining the characteristics of a good facilitator

▶ Explaining the purpose and setting the meeting ground rules

▶ Establishing the "parking lot"

▶ Negotiating the deliverables

▶ Designing the meeting process

- ▶ Exploring the facilitator tool kit
- ▶ Describing various tools, processes, and techniques of facilitation
- ▶ Reading the group—group dynamics and communication
- ▶ Doing group interventions—when and how
- ▶ Using flipcharts, PowerPoint, handouts
- ▶ Practicing hands-on facilitation—participants choose a facilitation tool to practice with the training participants and receive feedback from the group
- ▶ Using meeting evaluation tools

Following training, these new facilitators were paired with experienced facilitators and given opportunities to practice with several campus work teams. This group of volunteer facilitators and their trainers, known as the Facilitators Network, meets monthly to share experiences and discover new tools to include in their facilitation toolkit. The facilitators also have provided information to unit managers on the benefits of using facilitation (see <http://www.informationservices.ku.edu/facilitators/>). The use of the facilitators has increased slowly as leaders and managers experience the process and its results. In addition, the facilitators themselves have contributed to more effective group processes by using their facilitation skills in the groups in which they regularly participate.

One of our unit leaders recently pointed out another advantage: After a facilitator from another unit began to participate in meetings of his unit, the unit leader found that the facilitator was not only helping the unit with effective group processes but also learning about the unit. The facilitators thus are improving their ability to contribute to the big picture within Information Services thanks to the information and knowledge they gain by working in other parts of the organization. The facilitators have developed skill sets useful in direct facilitation, can contribute more to the collaborative work within their own units, and work successfully in other areas of Information Services. These advantages point to results that justify the resources invested.

Mentoring as a Key to Individual Learning

Mentoring programs offer an established, proven best practice to enhance organizational and individual learning. Given the variety of units and classifications of staff at KU, we chose to experiment with different types of mentoring programs. This section presents two programs: a one-to-one program offered to the professional librarians as part of the university faculty mentoring program, and a group mentoring program offered to managerial staff.

At KU, the provost's office requires each not-yet-tenured library faculty member to have an assigned mentor (as are not-yet-tenured faculty in all departments and schools). The mentor serves a variety of purposes, but in essence is another resource person that the newer faculty member can turn to for advice and coaching on career and job issues, including the promotion and tenure process. In recent years, the KU Libraries has investigated best practices in mentoring and strengthened its mentoring program.

In 2002, the dean of libraries appointed a task group to recommend ways to improve the existing, rather informal mentoring program in the libraries. The group engaged in a process to learn more about mentoring programs at other research libraries with faculty status (a particularly good one at Louisiana State University was found), completed a literature search for relevant research, talked with colleagues at other institutions, and assessed the needs of the libraries' faculty.[11] The dean and the library faculty governance group accepted the task group's recommendations, and the revamped mentoring program debuted with a daylong retreat facilitated by an outside consultant with special expertise in library mentoring programs. Initial mentor-mentee assignments were made by a four-person Mentoring Committee that recruited a pool of potential mentors for about a dozen untenured librarians and helped match mentee interests and needs with mentor interests and strengths.

During the first year of operation, the Mentoring Committee guided the program, met or communicated frequently with mentors and mentees, and made recommendations for improving the program. Improvements included giving supervisors, administrators, and the mentee more say in the selection of mentors; asking mentors and mentees to spend some time each year assessing how the relationship was working and whether it should continue; and identifying additional ways to stimulate discussions, both individual and group, between mentors and mentees. Plans for the third year of the program include an all-day session with our original outside facilitator to review our progress, explore ideas for further improvement, and improve coaching skills (see <http://www.lib.ku.edu/public/mentoring/>).

Another approach to mentoring, group mentoring, builds collaboration between mentors and mentees without the commitments required in one-on-one relationships. In 2002, KU began a group mentoring program for women within Information Services with the purpose of growing the professional skills of middle-level women managers (see <http://www.informationservices.ku.edu/mentoring/>). The goal is to provide support for women professionals and empower them to progress in their chosen career paths with a focus on what they found useful. Mentoring activities have included open group discussions, educational presentations from faculty and staff experts, and individual mentoring meetings. The group meetings have provided the opportunity for the mentees to receive a diversity of views from the mentors and from their own peers. These meetings developed a lateral network of relationships for the participants that have decreased the time spent by the mentors but increased the range of coaching available to the mentees. Participants have found that the mentoring activities provide an important source of trust, strong relationships, and interpersonal support.[12] Mentors are encouraged to take an educational approach to providing guidance and to share insights from their experiences. Mentees are encouraged to ask for the opportunities they need to grow their professional skills and to learn strategies for management of professional projects, employee issues, and interpersonal work relationships. The program is based on a curriculum focused on leadership and management skill sets, compiled with the assistance of KUHRPD.

Resources to Develop the Organizational Learning Infrastructure

A focus on employee development has always been essential for any organization. In recent years we have been particularly challenged to find resources for professional development (PD) as major technology projects have taken a large share of the overall budget, and PD can be one of the first items cut.[13] As Paul Gandel and Cynthia Golden explained in a recent *EDUCAUSE Quarterly* article, however, there are many ways to design and implement PD programs that do not require a large investment of financial resources.[14] One of the least expensive ways to fund a program is to take full advantage of the resources on your campus.

As KU began to develop the organizational learning infrastructure, clearly a major increase in monetary commitments was not realistic. Although we increased PD resources, much of the increase went to additional technical training and education in new technologies, which we considered a high priority. Therefore, we needed to find other ways of providing resources. Two strategies proved critical to our success: a partnership with the KU Human Resources Department Professional Development staff, and soliciting participation from faculty experts. We found common ground with the HR organizational development staff in their willingness to share their professional knowledge and offer customized programs for Information Services. They appreciated our willingness to learn and take a "train the trainers" approach to our programs so that the contact hours for their experts were reduced. This also provided great learning opportunities for members of the Information Services staff.

A somewhat unusual approach to resource allocation was our relationship with faculty experts. Mostly they were happy to donate their time as consultants because it gave them the opportunity to see their expertise applied in a functional setting. We also found that doing something meaningful for them in return turned out to be easy and fairly inexpensive. One of the most popular gestures was supplying a small grant for their travel in exchange for consultant time. We found this far less expensive than hiring outside consultants, and it had the additional benefit of developing faculty members' knowledge of Information Services work and our knowledge of their needs. We believe the future holds great promise for building on expertise found within the collaborative networks of the university, adding strength to our professional networks.

Conclusion

Our efforts to build an infrastructure within Information Services at KU to enhance employee learning and the organization as a whole has been a key factor in our organizational success. Building a consensus on values as a base to the infrastructure was an important first step. Educating leaders and managers about the day-to-day meaning of those values through the changing of individual behaviors began to alter the perspective of all employees. Using facilitation techniques improved group collaboration and allowed staff who became facilitators to improve their skill sets and learn about other units. The provision of mentoring programs has expanded thinking about PD and provided coaching for employee improvement.

Taking advantage of the resources readily available on the campus allowed us to build our programs in a cost-effective manner. The creation of the OD Group provided sustained leadership for the improvement and continued evaluation of the program. We hope our experiences focusing on these important human resource areas will serve as a catalyst to other information services organizations in higher education.

Endnotes

1. Marcus Buckingham, "The One Thing You Need to Know," 2004 EDUCAUSE Annual Conference General Session, October 21, 2004, Denver, Colorado.

2. Roger McDonald, "From Wires to Users," *EDUCAUSE Review*, vol. 39, no. 2 (March/April 2004), pp. 56–57, <http://www.educause.edu/LibraryDetailPage/666?ID=ERM0429>.

3. Jerry W. Gilley and Ann Maycunich, *Organizational Learning, Performance, and Change: An Introduction to Strategic Human Resource Development* (Cambridge, Mass.: Perseus Publishing, 2000).

4. Sheila Creth, "Optimizing Organization Design for the Future," *EDUCAUSE Quarterly*, vol. 23, no. 1 (2000), pp. 32–38, <http://www.educause.edu/LibraryDetailPage/666?ID=EQM0014>.

5. Wendell L. French and Cecil H. Bell, Jr., *Organization Development: Behavioral Science Interventions for Organization Improvement, 6th Edition* (Upper Saddle River, N.J.: Prentice Hall, 1999), pp. 25–26.

6. Denise Stephens and Keith Russell, "Organizational Development, Leadership, Change, and the Future of Libraries," *Library Trends*, vol. 53, no. 1 (Summer 2004), pp. 238–257, 241.

7. Organizational Development and Leadership, a special issue of *Library Trends* edited by Keith Russell and Denise Stephens, vol. 53, no. 1 (Summer 2004), pp. 1–264.

8. Chris Argyris and Donald A. Schon, *Organizational Learning II* (Reading, Mass.: Addison-Wesley, 1996), p. 20.

9. Shelley E. Phipps, "The System Design Approach to Organizational Development: The University of Arizona Model," *Library Trends*, vol. 53, no. 1 (Summer 2004), pp. 68–111.

10. Sam Kaner et al., *Facilitators Guide to Participatory Decision-Making* (Philadelphia: New Society Publishers, 1996).

11. For information about the Louisiana State University experience, see Lois Kuyper-Rushing, "A Formal Mentoring Program in a University Library: Components of a Successful Experiment," *Journal of Academic Librarianship*, vol. 27, no. 6 (November 2001), pp. 440–446. Other useful references on mentoring are two books by Lois J. Zachary, *The Mentor's Guide: Facilitating Effective Learning Relationships* (San Francisco: Jossey-Bass, 2000) and *Creating a Mentoring Culture: The Organization's Guide* (San Francisco: Jossey-Bass, 2005).

12. Judith A. Pirani, "IT Leadership Development: The University of Kansas Mentoring Program" (Boulder, Colo.: EDUCAUSE Center for Applied Research, research bulletin, issue 4, 2004), <http://www.educause.edu/LibraryDetailPage/666?ID=ERB0409>.

13. Lawrence C. Ragan, "Creative Strategies for Meeting the Needs of the Lifelong IT Professional," *EDUCAUSE Quarterly*, vol. 25, no. 2 (2002), pp. 58–61, <http://www.educause.edu/LibraryDetailPage/666?ID=EQM0228>.

14. Paul B. Gandel and Cynthia Golden, "Professional Development in Tough Financial Times," *EDUCAUSE Quarterly*, vol. 27, no. 1 (2004), pp. 45–48, <http://www.educause.edu/LibraryDetailPage/666?ID=EQM0416>.

About the Authors

Marilu Goodyear is associate professor of public administration at the University of Kansas. From 1999 to 2005, she was the vice provost for information services and CIO at the University of Kansas. In this role, she led all campus-wide software, hardware, and networking technology services, printing services, and the KU libraries. Goodyear serves as an EDUCAUSE Center for Advanced Research (ECAR) fellow. Her research areas are information policy, organizational change, and mentoring. Goodyear holds master's degrees in library and information science and public administration from the University of Missouri, as well as a doctorate in public administration from the University of Colorado.

Kathleen Ames-Oliver manages the Professional & Organizational Effectiveness Unit in the Department of Human Resources and Equal Opportunity at the University of Kansas, where she serves as a group facilitator and professional coach in a variety of areas including leadership, group facilitation, team and organizational effectiveness, change management, communications, coaching and mentoring, and conflict resolution. She holds degrees in performance theater and counseling psychology from the University of Missouri at Kansas City and has more than 15 years of experience working with individuals and groups in both business and academic settings.

Keith Russell is on the Libraries faculty at the University of Kansas. He has a joint appointment in the KU Department of Human Resources and Equal Opportunity, doing training, team building, facilitation, and other organizational development interventions. His research interests include best practices in healthy organizations, group facilitation and empowerment, and the practical and academic aspects of designing and using experiential exercises to enhance team effectiveness and change group behavior. Russell has an undergraduate degree in biology from Illinois State University and master's degrees in both botany and library science from the University of Illinois, Urbana–Champaign.

Part II:
The Individual Perspective

CHAPTER 4

Taking Control of Your Career

William F. Hogue
University of South Carolina

David W. Dodd
Xavier University

Career Management Equals Career Development

Your career should be something you manage, not something that manages you. If you're like most people, you'll spend more time on work than in any other waking activity for three or four decades in the prime of your life. Few endeavors are capable of providing more pleasure and fulfillment— or the opposite! But many of us fail to realize—or realize too late—that we can play a major role in creating positive career outcomes.

You can avoid that mistake. Start with a few questions. How might you assess your potential for leadership? How could you develop it? How do you know when you're ready for a bigger challenge? How can you strengthen and showcase your abilities and put yourself in the best position to compete for your ideal job? Where can you get good advice and counsel?

Answering these questions can help you manage your career more intelligently and yield a lifetime of professional satisfaction, excitement, and fulfillment. For some people, the greatest personal measure of career success is whether they've made a difference. Many of us work in higher education for precisely that reason—to make a difference in something we care about passionately. This chapter explores how career management and development can increase your satisfaction and fulfillment and perhaps even lead to that wonderful outcome.

It Takes Careful Planning

If all you need to know about real estate is "location, location, location," then all you need to know about career development is "planning, planning, planning." We schedule regular medical and dental checkups, take our cars in for periodic servicing, and manage our personal finances monthly, yet many of us pay little attention to systematic career development. How can you avoid that mistake and get started?

Self-assessment is a first step in career planning. A number of tools and techniques can help you better understand yourself and your abilities. An Internet search, for example, will return countless sites offering Keirsey, Myers-Briggs, and other self-assessment tools. One of the best sites we have found is <http://www.FastCompany.com>, which has tools and links to useful assessment resources. The Office of Personnel Management, the federal government's human resources agency, lists 27 desirable leadership competencies at <http://www.leadership.opm.gov/content.cfm?cat=LAW-CEL-FEI#key> and offers a rich set of self-assessment resource links at <http://www.leadership.opm.gov/knowlinks.cfm>. The National Association of College and University Business Officers (NACUBO) Web site at <http://www.nacubo.org/> includes a knowledge network for IT professionals that may help you better assess how your competencies map to those of your peers. Colleges and universities offer diverse resources for career planning and career development, including many opportunities for assessing interests and capabilities. Seminars, conferences, and institutes sponsored by EDUCAUSE and other professional associations offer additional opportunities to invest in career planning. Whatever mechanisms you choose, remember that self-assessment is the essential starting point for career planning.

Simple self-reflection is important, too. An interesting starting point for career planning, particularly for aspiring leaders, is the question of nature versus nurture. Are leaders born or developed? How much "raw material" must be present for a professional development process to succeed? Promotions don't make leaders—they merely fill positions. Have you thought through what is required of a leader, and your own potential to meet the demands of leadership?

Just about any bestseller about the characteristics of great leaders provides a laundry list of important leadership attributes. For purposes of illustration, we'll restrict our own list of examples to motivation, internal strength, and competitiveness, but any published list will do. The important thing is that you take your attributes list and do something with it.

Let's take motivation, for example. What drives you to develop your career? Money, prestige, authority, family, security, best use of your skills, escaping a career cul-de-sac, relocation to a better climate, altruism, or some combination of the above? This isn't a test with right and wrong answers—and nobody's recording grades—so be realistic. Trying to be something you aren't consumes an enormous amount of mental and emotional energy, and you can't sustain the effort for long. So take your time and consider your answer carefully: What's your motivation for developing your career?

The reason we include internal strength, or courage, on our short list of leadership attributes is simple: Successful IT leaders must be agents for change and continuous improvement. Change requires the strength and courage to progress in the face of resistance. That sometimes requires decisive—even courageous—action. We assume you have the intelligence required of a leader, but can you make tough decisions when you must?

Consider a final illustration from our short list: You must decide whether you have the competitiveness required of a leader. There is much to be said for working together to achieve the proverbial "win-win" situation, but competition surrounds us. Universities face stiff competition for students, faculty, resources, partnerships, and image. As a professional, you competed to win your present job, must compete to retain it, and will face even broader competition if you elect to move up to a higher level. You must be prepared to compete successfully and then to use resources available to help your institution compete effectively. Do you have the drive to compete? Answer the question for yourself, not for anyone else. In career development, you don't get any points for self-delusion!

Once you've written your own list of essential attributes, define your goal and conduct a systematic gap analysis of your attributes relative to that goal. For example, if your goal is to become a CIO at a major university, what education, experience, and personal qualities are generally required? A review of current and past online posted positions at EDUCAUSE, the *Chronicle of Higher Education*, and other national sites can be illuminating. Identifying a person you believe has the right stuff and listing his or her characteristics can also provide useful information. Then you have two questions before you that demand rigor in the answering: What qualities are employers looking for that you do not currently have, and how do you set a course of action to close that gap? More information to help you get started may be found at sites such as the Leadership Learning Community Web Site at

<http://www.leadershiplearning.org/>, the U.S. Geological Survey (USGS) Office of Employee Development at <http://training.usgs.gov/>, or the EDUCAUSE Resource Center at <http://www.educause.edu/resources>.

Closing the Gap: Enhancing Skills and Experience

All of us have gaps in skills and experience compared to that ideal résumé potential employers might desire. Are you aware of your gaps, and do you have a plan to close them? Conducting a gap analysis on yourself, especially if you seek the honest feedback of others, is a humbling but essential experience. You should be proud of your accomplishments, but this exercise is designed to expose your weaknesses and shortcomings, so hang on!

The position of CIO, for example, requires an array of skills and abilities. You must be adept at leadership, systems thinking, politics, fiscal management and budgeting, written and oral communication, strategic planning, and so forth. As discussed earlier, you can construct an inventory of these essential skills by reviewing job postings and examining the qualifications of successful and respected CIOs. You should look at your own professional qualifications and those required of positions you seek, and then identify differences between the two. That's an important achievement, but only part of the job. Now you have to decide how to close the gaps.

You can choose from a number of ways to acquire the education and experience needed. One of the most straightforward approaches is to take on additional responsibilities at work or in service organizations. For example, if you are relatively inexperienced in fiscal matters, you could get involved in budgeting or account management in your current job or in a local religious, civic, or nonprofit organization. Working at colleges and universities also provides wonderful opportunities for additional training. Taking a class in business or accounting might some day give you an edge over another applicant for a great job.

Another way to gain knowledge and credibility in a particular area is to become involved as a volunteer, speaker, teacher, or writer. It may sound foolhardy to participate when you have limited knowledge, but stay with it, and you'll inevitably learn—perhaps to the point of mastery. As a faculty member and friend once said, "If you want to gain credibility on a subject, become a speaker on that subject." Volunteering your time on committees is also an excellent way to explore new fields, gain credibility, and make important professional contacts. EDUCAUSE offers a number of volunteer opportunities, as do other professional, civic, and service organizations.

Overcoming shortcomings in your skills and experiences requires commitment and investment of time and effort. That often makes the difference between who will be qualified for opportunities when they arise and who will not.

What about moving to a new position altogether as a means of closing a professional qualification gap? Sometimes there is no better way to move up in your career than by moving on. Careful consideration may reveal that you have exhausted all reasonable possibilities for professional development where you are, or an opportunity may come along that represents a way to gain important skills and experience. One of the things that aspiring leaders must understand is the high probability of relocation at some point. If moving on to a new job in a new area is not something you are willing or able to do, you should realize this early and plan your career accordingly.

Suppose, though, you decide it is time to make a move. What then?

Evaluating Professional Opportunities

Professional opportunities should be approached carefully and from a strategic perspective. Not every opportunity for advancement represents a wise move, even if it offers more money, broader responsibility, or a fancier title. If you've been managing your career, you already should have a list of important questions to use in evaluating opportunities that arise. You'll develop your own set of questions, but these come immediately to mind:

▶ Are you ready for the opportunity? In other words, do your skill set and experience ensure a reasonable chance of success in the position?

▶ Does the position contribute substantially to additional professional development, particularly in priority areas you have already identified?

▶ Would the position lead to other opportunities later, either directly or indirectly?

Effective leaders ask their followers to stretch, to achieve goals that are challenging and seemingly out of reach. You might ask the same of yourself in the context of your career. There is nothing wrong with stretching to achieve those things that challenge you and require you to invest heavily of yourself to succeed.

It helps to remember that just because you can land a new job doesn't mean it is the right job and that it represents a good fit for you either personally or professionally. A widely held assumption in higher education is the "three-year rule," which essentially says that the minimum time you must spend in a position to ensure that it is viewed with legitimacy is three years. Those three years can pass very quickly in a position you enjoy and in which you achieve success. On the other hand, three years can seem an eternity in the wrong position or situation.

The path to your ideal job is rarely straight. Career development is more like sailing. It requires patience, a long-term view, and careful navigation in what is often a complex and changing environment. Tacking to one side or the other, the sailing equivalent of taking somewhat indirect approaches to a goal, is often the fastest course. It is sometimes wise to take what might appear to be a lateral position in order to gain the momentum needed to achieve your ultimate goal. For example, a CIO at a smaller school who lacks experience in a larger environment may elect to take an assistant or associate CIO job at a larger school for several years. Not all career moves are—nor should they be—upward. Career development is a journey.

At the same time, opportunities working part- or full-time in environments other than higher education may be very useful in helping you achieve an ultimate leadership position, such as CIO. Working or advising in business and industry, government, and nonprofits may be of great value. Experience transferred from other economic sectors or even other disciplines and professions may help higher education transform to meet the emerging challenges of the 21st century. One successful CIO at a medical university that includes a major teaching hospital left academia and spent the better part of a decade employed by a national, for-profit hospital system. His perspectives on issues ranging from budgeting and supply-chain management to staff development broadened considerably, and he has adapted and applied what he learned during this phase of his career to strengthen his current operation.

Don't discount a senior staff position as a rewarding step in career development. Leadership contributions are not always measured by the breadth of resources under your control. One colleague, for example, has contributed significantly to the body of knowledge in IT policy and law with little prior experience in IT. Another colleague coordinates rapidly evolving IT professional development programs for university scientists through a research advocacy organization. Both report at senior levels and are nationally visible and influential. Finding your perfect staff position may require a little finesse, but there's no better way to explore this option and learn about opportunities than to discuss it with your institutional and professional network.

As a final consideration, you may wish to create your own niche. Independent consulting, for example, is not reserved for those who want to remain active in the profession after retirement. Many areas in higher education IT would benefit from a new voice or an innovative approach. Once again, self-assessment is key. Do you have specialized and marketable skills that would generate sufficient income? Are you motivated and organized enough to run your own small business? Do you know how to create an effective and sustainable business plan? Review checklists for small business planning at sites such as <http://www.americanexpress.com/> for a reality check. Although genuine risks exist that you should not underestimate, opportunities for gaining both valuable skills and recognition abound in these special niches.

If you're contemplating a move of any kind, consider the following questions and advice from experienced colleagues from around the country:

▶ What opportunities do you have for advancement where you are now? Is someone in your way in your current location? For example, if you feel ready to be a CIO but your present CIO is performing well and shows no signs of leaving, you have a decision to make.

▶ If you want to move, examine context—the nature of the potential institution, its plans and prospects, where the position reports and who it influences, and resources (now and in the future). No university commits big bucks for anyone to come in and maintain the status quo. Where are the problems buried? What is your probability of success in the position? How big is the job, and how long will it remain interesting and challenging?

▶ Examine the community and the region, including cost-of-living and other quality-of-life indicators. A prospective 20 percent salary increase is not nearly so enticing if the cost of housing is 50 percent higher in a new location. Are there IT opportunities in higher education nearby so you won't have to relocate when looking for new challenges five years hence? There may be compelling reasons to take a position at an excellent university in a small, rural town in the Midwest. There may be different, but equally compelling, reasons to accept a position in a major metropolitan area that offers many diverse, long-term opportunities at different institutions without having to relocate.

▶ Consider the special challenges of families and two-career couples. Professional opportunities must be balanced with personal lives and commitment to others.

▶ Talk to colleagues about your options. Should you opt to apply for another position, never underestimate the power of a strong reference from a respected fellow professional.

▶ Move on gracefully. When you leave an institution, don't burn bridges. Be thoughtful and constructive in your exit interviews. Transitioning out is not a license to catalogue the flaws and failures of the individuals you worked with or the institution that paid you every month. Colleagues will remember how you left long after they've forgotten how you arrived.

Moving forward is the key. Positions and opportunities that provide needed skills and experience in particular environments, even if they do not take you straight to the goal, may well represent the fastest and surest course in career advancement. It takes judgment, self-awareness, patience, and sound navigation to recognize the possibilities. In almost all cases, opportunities are far better viewed in the perspective of professional development than professional advancement. Clearly, they are not always the same.

Career Development: Continuously Building Relationships and Optimizing Opportunities

Lamar Gordon, a very accomplished and highly regarded CIO at an elite university, faced his annual performance review. A conscientious man, he painstakingly compiled and organized the year's accomplishments and carefully wrote his division's goals and objectives for the coming year. He submitted his materials well in advance of the appointment with his superior, Executive Vice President Joe Swenson. The night before his appointment, Gordon spent more than an hour reviewing his materials and organizing his talking points.

The preparation paid off. The appointment went well. Swenson spent a little time probing a major project that was behind schedule and embroiled in difficult politics, but he generally applauded Gordon's leadership and fiscal prudence and the completion of several important projects. He concluded by promising budgetary and political support for next year's high-priority objectives. It was a very good meeting, Gordon felt.

As Gordon gathered his materials to leave, he asked, almost as an afterthought, "Joe, is there anything else I should be doing to help the university?"

Joe didn't hesitate. "Lamar," he said, "you need to make friends."

The names and incidental details are fictitious, but the main story is true. And the message is powerful. Joe was not suggesting that Lamar Gordon improve his social life. He was advising him to develop deeper relationships with key constituents who influenced the university's budget and strategic decisions.

Over the following year, Gordon personally visited each dean and vice president to explain—in nontechnical language—the value of proposed new IT initiatives to the university. He patiently listened to grievances old and new and paid particular attention to relatively minor but annoying hot-button issues that could be solved quickly by a focused IT response. He beefed-up VIP service so that busy executive offices with computing and networking problems or with specialized applications received fast, high-quality attention. And he placed renewed emphasis on direct customer engagement as a requirement for all of his directors and managers. Not surprisingly, new IT initiatives received broader executive support than usual during budget hearings at the end of the year.

Making friends is not generally a topic in executive education curricula, but it is one of the most important areas of career development. Strong collegial relationships built on mutual trust and an understanding of each other's high-priority issues are essential for success in your current role, and—inside and outside the institution—for building your future career.

Making friends—engaging people on issues of importance to them or to you—is sometimes described disparagingly as politics. Politics is not a dirty word. In the classical sense, politics is simply the tactics, techniques, and methods used in managing an organization. And political opportunity can come in unexpected places, such as graduation ceremonies.

One CIO reported that he attends at least six graduations each year at his large state university. "First," he said, "it reminds me why I'm here. I love being part of the celebration of intellectual achievement. I put on my doctoral robes and [proceed] past the faculty and students as a member of the platform party. It's especially important that the faculty see my commitment to what they're doing. Besides that, it's fun! So many happy families!"

There's additional political value to this participation, the CIO noted:

> Some people might think attending graduation is a waste of my time. But the president and provost, all the deans, and many members of the Board of Trustees are in the platform party. For about 30 minutes before and after the processional, there's plenty of time to mix and mingle and have informal conversations. Everyone's relaxed. It's important for these folks to know me, decide whether they can trust me, talk about what's on their mind. They'll remember the person behind the text the next time our strategic plans are up for review. I make an effort to have cordial and informed relationships with all of my key customers and partners. That can make all the difference.

Make Career Planning a Habit

You've probably figured out by now that planning your career and your professional development is a continuous cycle that involves periodically assessing where you are, reflecting on your goals, and plotting new directions and strategies as necessary. Just as you schedule time to review your retirement portfolio now and then, schedule a quiet time at least once a year to review your current situation, assess your short- and long-term goals, and adjust your roadmap.

Whether you think you'll be moving soon or you're committed to your present institution for a lifetime, your résumé or CV merit the same regularly scheduled attention as the rest of your career development strategies. Your résumé is your marketing tool. It tells both friends and strangers what you've accomplished and gives them clues about what you may be capable of accomplishing in the future. It's surprisingly easy to forget invited presentations, development seminars, community service, committee assignments, or even awards and recognitions if you wait until months or years later to add them to the written record of your accomplishments.

A final thought: Career planning is a continuous process and not a discrete event. There is wisdom in Dwight Eisenhower's statement that the planning process is far more valuable than the plan itself. Professional development plans must be flexible and responsive to changing opportunities and challenges throughout your career. We live in a very dynamic higher education ecosystem where adaptation has become the norm. Make continuous planning a habit, and you'll give yourself the gift of a great opportunity to watch your career thrive.

About the Authors

William F. Hogue has been vice president for information technology and CIO for the eight campuses of the University of South Carolina since 2000. His duties include development of IT and distance education strategy, policy, and practice for some 43,000 students, faculty, and staff at two-year, four-year, and research institutions within the USC system. Prior to assuming his current role, Hogue held IT leadership positions at Vanderbilt University, the University of Wisconsin System, and MIT. He holds undergraduate and master's degrees from the University of South Carolina and a doctorate from Harvard University.

David W. Dodd is vice president for information resources and CIO at Xavier University, where he has comprehensive leadership responsibility for IT, the university library, Web development, instructional technology, and strategic information resources. He is charged with the development of an integrated, systematic, and holistic model of information resources and services to support the university. Prior to joining Xavier, he held IT leadership positions at the University of South Carolina at Spartanburg, the University of North Carolina at Wilmington, and the University of North Carolina at Charlotte. Dodd holds a master's degree from the State University of New York in Binghamton and is completing a PhD in educational leadership and policy.

CHAPTER 5

The Importance of Mentors

Susan E. Metros
The Ohio State University

Catherine Yang
EDUCAUSE

Mentoring is a professional activity, a trusted relationship, a meaningful commitment. The origins of mentoring can be traced back to ancient Greece as a technique to impart to young men important social, spiritual, and personal values. Mentoring as we know it today is loosely modeled on the historical craftsman/apprentice relationship, where young people learned a trade by shadowing the master artisan. In the mid-70s, corporate America redefined mentoring as a career development strategy. The concept of mentoring faculty and administrators is relatively new to higher education and rare in information technology circles, where staff professional development often takes the form of technical manuals and certifications. It is precisely this type of support organization, however, that needs a strong foundation of mentoring to build and retain a healthy workforce that can react quickly to change and can develop, adapt, and regenerate itself over time.

Mentoring relationships range from loosely defined, informal collegial associations in which a mentee learns by observation and example to structured, formal agreements between expert and novice co-mentors where each develops professionally through the two-way transfer of experience and perspective. Whether the relationship is deemed formal or informal, the goal of mentoring is to provide career advice as well as both professional and personal enrichment. For this chapter, we define a mentoring relationship as helping and supporting people to "manage their own learning in order to maximize their professional potential, develop their skills, improve their performance, and become the person they want to be."[1]

The Need to Develop IT Leaders in Higher Education

The seminal EDUCAUSE Center for Applied Research (ECAR) study on information technology leadership in higher education[2] warns that while the majority of IT professionals surveyed find working in higher education to be rewarding, the next generation of potential IT leaders is dwindling. The up-and-comers perceive campus IT as a cool climate for innovation yet lacking in a diverse workforce. Perhaps most strikingly, they find the CIO career path too hefty a personal commitment. This finding is particularly ominous because over a quarter of all respondents planned to retire within five years or less, leaving a gaping need for new leadership. The report makes two recommendations to alleviate this problem: looking for leaders in nontraditional places, and identifying and mentoring promising candidates.

Organizations' Responsibilities

College campuses, while expert at offering traditional education to a diverse student clientele, are not as skilled in identifying and supporting their own staff's professional development (PD) needs. Few institutions dedicate the time and resources required to offer formal mentoring programs to their IT staff. Those that do usually target specific groups of employees—usually women or minorities. As one excellent example, Information Services at the University of Kansas sponsors the Women's Mentoring Program (http://www.informationservices.ku.edu/mentoring), which provides support for middle-level women managers, empowering them to progress in their chosen career paths and grow their professional skills. Professional organizations such as EDUCAUSE facilitate mentoring by offering a variety of PD programs and leadership institutes for IT staff; indeed, many of these programs initiate mentoring relationships.

While most of the popular books on leadership expound on mentoring, you cannot learn to be a mentor or mentee by reading a book or following cookie-cutter leadership advice. One size does not fit all, particularly in higher education IT organizations. Technology is constantly evolving, making mentoring difficult because leadership responsibilities constantly shift to stay abreast of change. The employees of these organizations work hard to serve the needs of their academic community and must often react quickly to emergencies with constrained resources. Mentoring programs would appear to be luxuries in this fast-paced and unpredictable work environment.

For mentoring to effect institutional change in higher education, it must be more than informal or spontaneous. The leadership within an institution must first recognize and identify the need for mentoring, and then plan, develop, support, and promote a program that directly addresses specific workforce gaps—both current and future. Regardless, whether the leadership at an institution recognizes and supports mentoring, a staff member's career can benefit from a mentoring relationship, even if not officially sanctioned.

Goals of a Mentoring Relationship

An essential first step in a successful mentoring relationship is for both the mentor and mentee to identify, define, and honestly articulate their common and individual goals and motives. Does the mentor want to eventually delegate a portion of his or her job responsibilities to the mentee? Or is the mentor secretly developing a succession plan? Does the mentee envision mastering their "craft" or transitioning away from hands-on work to build management and leadership skills? Is the mentee planning to use the mentoring experience to progress within the organization or to seek employment elsewhere? Are both looking to give back to the organization and make the work environment a better place for all, or is mentoring a stepping-stone to personal and professional growth?

Based on interviews with three senior administrators at the University of South Carolina, co-mentors William Hogue and Ernest Pringle[3] developed a "work in progress" set of Mentor Guiding Principles:

▶ **Strive for mutual benefits.** The relationship should be defined from the beginning as mutually beneficial. Each participant has committed to the relationship by choice. Each should openly share his or her goals for the relationship and work collaboratively to help achieve them.

▶ **Agree on confidentiality.** Maintaining an environment of confidentiality is a critical component in building trust between the participants. Without a mutually understood ability to speak freely as the situation warrants, the relationship is unlikely to reach its full potential.

▶ **Commit to honesty.** The participants should be willing to candidly share what they expect to gain from the relationship and their vision for getting there. They should be prepared to offer frank feedback as appropriate, even if the feedback is critical.

▶ **Listen and learn.** Mutual benefit and honesty can only be achieved when both members feel their viewpoints are heard and respected. Mentors, especially, need to remember that the relationship is not primarily about them. Co-mentors should not be intimidated or made to feel their views are not valued.

▶ **Build a working partnership.** Consider structuring a working partnership that includes project consultation or active collaborations rooted in the common ground of shared professional goals. These collaborations can lead to discoveries about each participant's preferred working style, daily obligations, and professional aspirations.

▶ **Lead by example.** Actions create the most lasting impression.

▶ **Be flexible.** It might help for a mentoring relationship to have defined goals, but the process may be as important—or more so—than the goals.

Types of Mentoring Relationships

There are many types of mentoring relationships, and it is essential to understand the differences and nuances prior to cultivating and entering into a mentoring agreement. What characteristics do you seek—formal or informal, mandatory or optional, short term or long term?

One of the most important distinctions is whether the mentoring relationship is considered formal or informal. Most mentoring relationships sit somewhere on a continuum between these two extremes. Formal mentoring relationships are often mandatory—leadership assigns mentors to new hires or promising candidates for promotion. The meetings are scheduled, tracked, documented, and evaluated based on clearly articulated goals and milestones. Informal mentoring relationships are more spontaneous and based on loosely defined results. In fact, many mentoring relationships, while fulfilling the PD needs of the participants, are not acknowledged as such. Often the mentee enters an informal mentoring relationship because of an intrinsically motivated need to do better. Whereas formal mentoring relationships tend to be more hierarchical, with seniority, status, and even age defining the mentor/protégé relationship, informal mentoring is more likely based on trust or admiration.

Another important attribute to clarify at the outset is whether the relationship is short term or long term. A short-term mentorship usually addresses a specific set of needs, while a long-term mentoring relationship might fulfill broad-based PD requirements over the course of a career.

Despite the benefits of mentoring throughout a career, the skills and type of advice needed inevitably change over time. At the beginning of a career, a more job-specific mentor may be appropriate.[4] For example, a suitable mentor might be someone who is highly technically skilled and can provide advice on ways to become more technically proficient. As organizational roles evolve into more supervisory capacities, mentors who can provide more career-related, organizational, political, and managerial skills development can be beneficial. In the later part of a career, retirement and succession planning guidance may become more important. Longtime employees also might benefit from what Jack Welch, former CEO of General Electric, called "reverse mentoring"—partnering with someone from a younger generation to share expertise, update skills, and gain a fresh perspective.

Types of Mentors

Different mentoring relationships generate a whole host of mentor types and styles.

▶ **The wise leader** is someone who through executive title, seniority, or status within the organization has reached the pinnacle of his or her career and is worthy of and willing to impart knowledge and wisdom to others in the organization. Often natural leaders, these politically astute individuals exude a certain air of confidence and innately understand and have thrived within the organization's culture and practices. While most of their mentoring relationships are formally arranged, wise leaders have been known to take on protégés in informal apprenticeships.

▶ **The life coach** is a professional mentor, often in the organization's human resources division or an outside consultant. Staff looking to change jobs or careers often hire life coaches outside the work environment to evaluate their performance, prepare for new career opportunities, or simply set and achieve personal goals. These relationships tend to be short term with a targeted and prioritized set of objectives. While life coaching usually happens in a face-to-face environment, more and more life coaches are offering their services virtually—over the telephone or the Internet.

▶ **The teacher** could be an educator, working with current or past students to build their professional talents and skills, or someone who assumes the "honorary" role of teacher—promoting learning and growth by imparting knowledge, debating ideas, or recommending resources. A teaching relationship might be officially sanctioned, such as enrolling for independent study, or as informal as dropping by during office hours for a chat.

▶ **Peer mentors** participate in informal relationships in which colleagues or friends pair up to help each other grow within an organization. They might team up to gain professional development experience, share networking contacts, or simply support each other's career path choices.

- **The confidante** is not so much a mentor as someone to use as a touchstone or sounding board. It is helpful in both healthy and dysfunctional work environments to have a confidante with whom to bat ideas around, air frustrations, request reality checks, and seek advice.
- **The self-help mentor** takes the form of books, manuals, articles, checklists, software, Web sites, and so forth that provide proven formulas or step-by-step advice on how to grow professionally. While not a substitute for the real thing, some of these popular resources are useful in helping an employee map a career path and/or lay a foundation for future mentoring relationships.
- **The inner mentor** is the internal voice that calls upon intuition to glean and mold life experiences into a personalized leadership philosophy. This nontraditional self-mentoring approach takes into account past experiences, current competencies, and future potential. The first step is to conduct a life experience inventory, identifying experiences that might hold leadership potential. It is the deconstruction—the picking apart—of these experiences to reveal underlying values and beliefs that will translate into a customized set of leadership principles.[5] The process of mentoring yourself is difficult—it takes concentration, self-reflection, and the ability to trust your own instincts.

Mentoring Phases

The literature is crowded with examples of mentoring models. Kathy Kram[6] divided mentoring relationships into four phases—initiation, cultivation, separation, and redefinition. William Gray[7] envisioned a five-step mentor/protégé relationship—prescriptive, persuasive, collaborative, confirmative, and successful. Lois Zachary[8] cycled through four phases—prepare, negotiate, enable, and close. We have distilled these models and others down to four distinct stages—identify, negotiate, facilitate, and graduate.

Identify

In finding a mentor, it is important to establish the goals of the mentorship and the core competencies needed for effectiveness in present and future positions. Identifying an appropriate mentor and objectives is critical to successful career planning. (See Table 1.) For example, a new campus IT manager hired from industry probably will need help acclimating to the culture and politics of higher education. In this case, it would be wise to seek a successful mentor who has a deep understanding of how the institution works and of the historical characteristics for managerial excellence within the organization.

Table 1. Identify Phase Responsibilities

Mentor's Responsibilities	Mentee's Responsibilities
Have a clear understanding of your motivation for becoming a mentor	Have a clear understanding of your motivation for wanting to be mentored
Agree to mentor based on a realistic assessment of your skills and leadership experience	Select a mentor based on preestablished criteria relevant to your career goals
Be open to mentoring individuals from outside your discipline	Broaden your search for a mentor to include nontraditional fields and organizations

Potential mentors can be found in a variety of ways. A few large institutions have formal mentoring programs. Others have formal, IT-specific mentoring programs. An organization's human resources department can often provide information on both internal and external mentoring opportunities. Outside the organization, professional associations such as EDUCAUSE, the American Society for Training and Development (ASTD), and various other technical and local networking groups can help locate potential mentors. Another method is using mailing lists and online resources to identify people with specific expertise and experience. Finally, think creatively in identifying mentors. Ask friends, family, and colleagues for personal referrals. Advice can be found anywhere, not just in one field or institution.

While most mentoring relationships take place within the same organization, no steadfast rule says a mentor or mentee cannot come from beyond the boundaries of the discipline, division, or even the institution, especially as you advance in your career. This practice is more common in smaller organizations where mentors may not be as plentiful or diverse. IT support often spans numerous units of an organization, so mentoring relationships might pair central support staff with decentralized staff. Universities also employ a broad range of professional staff, so it might be wise for IT professionals to choose a mentor from another area such as the office of business and finance or the college of education, depending on which professional development gaps they hope to address.

While most mentor/mentee relationships involve two individuals, choosing multiple mentors, simultaneously or over a period of time, might prove beneficial. IT is complex and multifaceted, and a network of mentors makes it easier for the mentee to adapt to change and gain a diverse portfolio of knowledge quickly. Also, new research supports building "relationship constellations," a theory espousing the advantages of a protégé cultivating developmental networks comprised of multiple mentors.[9]

Another way to build a mentoring relationship is to partner with a colleague in choosing a mentor together. This "doubling up" eases the mentor's time commitment, and the mentee partner brings a different perspective to the table, broadening the scope of discussion. Use caution when participating in group mentoring programs, however, because the relationship of one mentor to many mentees does not always allow participants to address their individual goals.

Negotiate

Zachary[10] labeled the negotiating phase of the mentoring relationship as the "business phase." The mentoring partners must agree on the goals and outcomes, decide on ground rules, work out the details and logistics, and develop a mentoring plan complete with criteria for success. While formal mentoring programs might require a memorandum of understanding or even a signed contact, the negotiating phase is really about managing expectations, creating a shared understanding, and building a foundation of trust. (See Table 2.)

Table 2. Negotiate Phase Responsibilities

Mentor's Responsibilities	Mentee's Responsibilities
Have a clear understanding of your expectations for your mentee and the ensuing relationship	Have a clear understanding of your expectations for your mentor and the ensuing relationship
Clearly communicate your expectations	Clearly communicate your expectations
Be flexible—be willing to alter your expectations and change your plans	Be flexible—be willing to alter your expectations and change your plans
Have a plan (formal or informal) with milestones and defined deliverables	Have a plan (formal or informal) with milestones and defined deliverables
Codevelop an exit strategy	Codevelop an exit strategy
Try to adapt your feedback to your mentee's learning style	Inform your mentor of your preferred learning style
Be realistic about the time commitment to successfully oversee the relationship	Be realistic about the time commitment to do homework and self-reflection

Facilitate

The facilitation phase makes up the bulk of the mentoring relationship: the mentoring plan is implemented, and the relationship with the mentor is developed. (See Table 3.) For a mentor, Patricia Battin reminds us, the facilitation phase "means conscious tailoring of opportunities for individuals that require them to stretch—and then helping them do it."[11] For the mentee, this phase can be difficult, but ultimately rewarding—it means recognizing your strengths and weaknesses and addressing them through appropriate actions and opportunities.

Table 3. Facilitate Phase Responsibilities

Mentor's Responsibilities	Mentee's Responsibilities
Advise, don't dictate	Actively listen and contribute to the conversations
Advise on what you know; admit what you don't know or refer to others	Understand your mentor will not have all of the answers—be willing to look them up
Provide relevant examples and resources	Access resources—do your homework
Recognize your mentee's weaknesses but build on his or her strengths	Acknowledge your weaknesses but build on your strengths
Give constructive criticism	Accept and reflect on constructive criticism
Don't shy away from difficult conversations	Don't shy away from difficult conversations
Periodically evaluate progress and reassess the relationship	Periodically evaluate progress and reassess the relationship
Celebrate successes	Celebrate successes
Be reliable	Be reliable

Graduate

Once the mentoring relationship has been established and fostered, it is important to understand the parameters for when the association should change or end. (See Table 4.) Ending a mentoring relationship does not mean it has failed. Often,

Table 4. Graduate Phase Responsibilities

Mentor's Responsibilities	Mentee's Responsibilities
Be sensitive as to when the relationship has run its course	Be sensitive as to when the relationship has run its course
After mentoring relationship is finished, follow up on successes	Provide mentor with updates after mentoring relationship is finished
Provide a summative evaluation of the experience	Provide a summative evaluation of the experience
Don't forget to say thank you	Don't forget to say thank you and give credit where credit is due
Mark the graduation with a celebration	Mark the graduation with a celebration
Repeat the mentoring process with others	Give back to the profession and volunteer to mentor others

it simply means that the initial goals of the mentorship have been attained, and it is time to "graduate" and move on.

When ending a mentoring relationship, remember to thank a mentor for the knowledge and time provided. In the ensuing years, communicate your career progression. A mentoring relationship often evolves into a long-term professional friendship.

Sometimes, after a mentoring relationship begins, it may become apparent that the mentor chosen is not a good match for the mentee's PD needs. Perhaps the mentor has extenuating circumstances (for example, increased workload or family issues), or the participants simply cannot communicate effectively. In these cases, it is best for the two to have an honest conversation as to what is working and what is not working; if mentor and mentee cannot reconcile the differences, they should mutually agree to terminate the relationship.

Politics of Mentoring

It is important to address the obvious—and not so obvious—workplace politics associated with mentoring. First, the choice of a mentor can be tricky. Will a professional or personal relationship be damaged if the prospective mentor turns down the request? Will a potential mentor perceive the request as an honor or as an obligation? Will the mentor's own sense of security be threatened by an ambitious mentee who might compete for future positions? Does the mentee understand how others in the organization will perceive his or her choice of mentor? Is the mentor well regarded within the organization and within the broader profession? Is the mentor's network of colleagues comprised of respected leaders? If the mentor fails professionally, will the mentee also fail by association?

Both mentor and mentee must consider others' perceptions of equity issues. While mentoring relationships between individuals of different generations, ethnic backgrounds, cultures, color, and special needs are encouraged in higher education, mentoring relationships between genders and between individuals with same-sex orientation are sometimes held to a different standard, with potential criticism exacerbated by the power differential often associated with mentoring. Ultimately, distrust of such mentoring relationships is almost always based on misguided perceptions, bigotry, lack of knowledge, or pettiness. The mentor and mentee must determine the risk and decide what is best for their professional growth. Note, however, that the examples provided throughout this chapter may not be appropriate for members of certain religions or cultures where mentoring relationships might be perceived as an improper activity between individuals of different status, gender, or other characteristics.

Conclusion

This chapter serves as an introduction to the concepts of mentoring, particularly for those in higher education IT organizations. Every career and mentorship is unique, and may have different criteria and characteristics. Recognizing that professional development through mentorship can be highly beneficial to both mentor and mentee, mentoring is a critical element in preparing higher education leaders of the future. As Patricia Battin noted in her acceptance speech for the 1996 CAUSE Award for Exemplary Leadership and Information Technology Excellence,

> Mentorship represents an individual commitment to seeking out, identifying, and developing in a variety of ways the leaders of the future—people who have the creativity, the intellect, the conceptual skills, and the personal qualities necessary to provide true transformational leadership in the challenging, ever-changing, and fluid environment of contemporary higher education.[12]

Endnotes

1. Eric Parsloe, *Coaching, Mentoring, and Assessing* (London: Kogan Page, 1992).

2. Richard N. Katz and Gail Salaway, "Information Technology Leadership in Higher Education: The Condition of the Community Key Findings" (Boulder, Colo.: EDUCAUSE Center for Applied Research, January 2004), <http://www.educause.edu/LibraryDetailPage/666?ID=EKF0401>.

3. William F. Hogue and Ernest M. Pringle, "What's Next After You Say Hello: First Steps in Mentoring," *EDUCAUSE Quarterly*, vol. 28, no. 2 (2005), pp. 50–52, <http://www.educause.edu/LibraryDetailPage/666?ID=EQM0525>.

4. Gene Spencer and Cynthia Golden, "Mentors: Making a Difference for Tomorrow's Leaders," *EDUCAUSE Quarterly*, vol. 26, no. 2 (2003), pp. 51–53, <http://www.educause.edu/LibraryDetailPage/666?ID=EQM0326>.

5. Susan E. Metros, "A Heart to Heart on Leadership: How to Use Your Life Experiences to Become a Better Leader," *Association of College and Research Libraries College and Research Library News*, vol. 66, no. 6 (June 2005), pp. 447–450, <http://www.ala.org/ala/acrl/acrlpubs/crlnews/backissues2005/June05/hrttohrt.htm>.

6. Kathy E. Kram, "Phases of the Mentor Relationship," *Academy of Management Journal* vol. 26, no. 4 (1985), pp. 608–624.

7. William A. Gray, *Custom Designing Planned Mentoring Programs to Meet Contextual Needs* (Vancouver, B.C.: International Centre for Mentoring, 1988).

8. Lois J. Zachary, *The Mentor's Guide: Facilitating Effective Learning Relationships* (San Francisco: Jossey-Bass, 2000).

9. Monica C. Higgins and Kathy E. Kram, "Reconceptualizing Mentoring at Work: A Developmental Network Perspective," *Academy of Management Review*, vol. 26, no. 2 (April 2001), pp. 264–288.

10. Zachary, op. cit.

11. Patricia Battin, "Diversity and Leadership: Mentoring Builds Leaders of the Future," *CAUSE/EFFECT*, vol. 20, no. 1 (Spring 1997), pp. 15–17, <http://www.educause.edu/LibraryDetailPage/666?ID=CEM9715>.

12. Ibid.

About the Authors

Susan E. Metros is deputy CIO and executive director for e-learning at The Ohio State University. She also holds a faculty appointment as professor of design technology. As deputy CIO, she is responsible for leading the academic community in appropriately using technology-enhanced teaching and learning, both on campus and at a distance. In her role as educator and designer, she teaches within the visual communication curriculum and has served as principal designer on several international award-winning interactive multimedia and Web-based projects.

Catherine Yang is director of information technology and strategy at EDUCAUSE, where her responsibilities include oversight of IT and content strategy. Previously, she was director of client services at Bentley College and held a number of positions at Brown University. Yang holds a bachelor's in biology from Brown University.

CHAPTER 6

The Profession Needs You: Engagement as Professional Development

Cynthia Golden
EDUCAUSE

Dan Updegrove
The University of Texas at Austin

Many of us look at the chance to attend a training session, a conference, or a lecture as a wonderful opportunity to get out of the office, make new connections, engage with colleagues, and learn and reflect in an environment removed from the day-to-day pressures of campus IT life. We often return to campus with new ideas, feeling rejuvenated and ready to tackle the next big thing. Even reading an article or participating in a Webcast can be stimulating and give us new insights into our work. These positive experiences are not only valuable personal and professional activities but also directly benefit our institutions through an infusion of fresh energy and ideas and validation of current effective practice.

What about taking that next step? Could you be the person leading the discussion session at an upcoming conference or talking about a new project as part of a panel presentation? Many professional conferences, whether face-to-face or online events, organized by professional staff or grassroots efforts, solicit ideas and submissions for conference presentations and have committees of volunteers from the community who plan the event and create the program. Both print and Web-based journals have editorial committees that recruit and review articles written by colleagues. Might you consider writing an article about how your campus has addressed a pressing problem? Professional associations engage members in multiple types of advisory, planning, and program delivery capacities. Have you thought about sharing your work? Serving on a committee? Blogging about your professional specialty? If you have, you are already experiencing some of the rewards of getting involved in the profession. If you haven't, you might want to think about why you should. This chapter gives you some compelling reasons to become actively involved.

Stay Current in a Dynamic Field

I skate to where the puck will be. —Wayne Gretzky

IT in higher education is a fast-moving landscape of innovative products and services; new, merged, and defunct vendors; novel pedagogies; and changing business practices. Keeping pace with technology is necessary but not sufficient, since technologies often have adoption rates in academe that differ from the commercial and consumer mainstream. In some cases—TCP/IP and the Internet, the Macintosh, broadband in residences—education has been an early adopter, whereas we have lagged in deployment of security and other technologies. Our special challenge is understanding which technologies best suit the needs, budgets, and cultures of colleges and universities—the shape and surface of our hockey rinks, as it were.

Fortunately, our profession has two attributes that make this challenge tractable. The first is a broad continuum of expertise and commitment to technology leadership across higher education. Some institutions have long been committed to pioneering technology development and application, and others have recently identified IT leadership as a high priority. Indeed, some universities have dedicated units that track—and develop—advanced technology. The second attribute is a remarkable spirit of openness and information sharing, even among institutions competing fiercely for the brightest scholars and best athletes. This openness is manifest as IT leaders publish their work, present at conferences and seminars, host campus visits, and serve as advisors to colleagues from other institutions. Formal and informal opportunities for learning abound.

Broaden Your Perspective

The real voyage of discovery consists not in seeking new lands, but in seeing with new eyes. —Marcel Proust

Breakthrough ideas are not the exclusive domain of the most technologically advanced, research-intensive, or wealthiest institutions, of course. The ubiquity and declining cost of technology, the broad reach of the Internet, and the universal commitment to teaching, scholarship, and service provide fertile ground for exemplary applications of IT on most campuses. Moreover, business as usual in one department or institution may look like a "killer app" to someone seeing it for the first time, perhaps in a totally different context.

The University of Texas at Austin (UT Austin) is in the process of repurposing a large, centrally located building that once served primarily as an undergraduate library. The planning team, in search of a new vision for supporting 21st-century learning, visited not only campus libraries and learning commons but also MIT's Stata Center, Penn State's Information Sciences and Technology Building, Stanford's Wallenberg Hall, and Seattle's Experience Music Project. Learning from such visits can take the form of notes, photos, videos, and—notably—interviews with planners and users, whose experiences and insights can inform our work.

The value of these interchanges is not limited to the article reader, seminar attendee, or campus visitor, however. Many writers and presenters have discovered that the discipline of organizing one's thoughts for a new audience—and answering their questions—results in a more complete and coherent understanding of their topic.

Make Professional Contacts

It's not what you know, it's who you know (and how fast you can reach them using their preferred communications medium). —Anonymous

Assembling all the relevant information to enable an optimal decision is a fine theoretical construct, albeit one rarely experienced in practice. More typical is the requirement to speak with a reporter this afternoon, have a recommendation by Friday, or get the course management system back online, pronto. At such times published articles and Web searches may be much less helpful than professional colleagues, be they across campus, at other institutions, in industry, or on staff at associations. Contacting them can yield wise counsel, options you hadn't considered, and perhaps even an offer of assistance.

Savvy professionals communicate frequently through e-mail, phone, instant messaging (IM), campus lunch meetings, and conference hallway chats. They know how to reach key colleagues and their trusted assistants, they make themselves available to others, and they follow up on commitments, whether to call back with an answer or "summarize the results for the list." While a cold call to an expert in the field can sometimes be fruitful, most of us are more comfortable contacting people we know. Can your colleague in the School of Business loan you a server for a week? Has anyone in your peer group had this sort of request from the provost? Developing such a network of trusted and trusting colleagues is one of the most important strategies for professional success.

Gain Recognition for Your Work and Your Institution

Death most resembles a prophet who is without honor in his own land or a poet who is a stranger among his people. —Kahlil Gibran

Completing a challenging project on time and on budget is its own reward, but receiving recognition from peers can be immensely satisfying as well. The converse of seeking advice and exemplars for your efforts is having others address such questions to you—having you and your institution viewed as leaders. Interest, acclaim, and visits from other institutions can also increase satisfaction in both the project team and the user community. Of course, this can mean taking on the additional challenge of writing a paper or submitting a conference proposal, sometimes in midproject when 80 percent of the resources are depleted, and only 20 percent of the work is done!

Numerous other benefits accompany external recognition, ranging from kudos on annual performance reviews to institutional public relations payoffs. Speakers at conferences tend to meet many more people than those in the audience, and they often receive invitations to participate in other professional activities. Back on campus, a widely lauded success can make it easier to garner financial and political support for the next initiative and, quite possibly, attract interest from internal or external collaborators. Perhaps most important, over the long term, you have contributed to the accumulated experience, best practice, and insight that define the profession.

Serve the Community

Everybody can be great because everybody can serve. —Martin Luther King, Jr.

Fortunately, IT in colleges and universities attracts many bright and dedicated professionals. Most would admit, however, that the pace of change, escalating and diverse service demands, and constrained resources make this a remarkably demanding and stressful field. Longtime university CIO Ken King may have been exaggerating only slightly when he asserted, "Higher education sets the out-of-control standard to which other sectors aspire!" All of us, newcomers and veterans alike, come to depend on our colleagues for sage counsel, examples of best practices, and insights not learned the hard way. Such a repository of great ideas and helpful colleagues cannot exist, of course, without contributors—those willing to give back to the community.

Such service takes many forms: posting a reply on a peer list server, serving on a conference program committee, or hosting a visit from colleagues from another campus. Established professional associations, such as ACUTA (http://www.acuta.org) and EDUCAUSE (http://www.educause.edu), provide numerous well-structured and valuable venues for contributing and benefiting—seminars, conferences, publications, committees, task forces, mailing lists, and blogs. (See the sidebar "Navigating Professional Associations and Societies.")

Occasions arise, however, when no formal organization is positioned to respond to the community's need. For example, constructing and operating advanced state and regional optical networks in support of research and education fell outside the purview of existing organizations in some parts of the country, so IT leaders created new organizations, such as Florida LambdaRail and Texas's Lonestar Education and Research Network (LEARN). More recently, the impact of hurricanes Katrina and Rita precipitated a wide range of responses from campus IT, from establishing emergency Web sites and call centers for affected campuses to provisioning e-mail kiosks and building databases of evacuees and volunteers in campus and civic shelters.

Develop Leadership Skills

If your actions inspire others to dream more, learn more, do more, and become more, you are a leader. —John Quincy Adams

Anyone has the potential to be a leader. In fact, the merged IT/library organization at Bucknell University has incorporated an expectation of leadership at all levels in their value statements and in all aspects of their work. We've all seen people who are not in positions of power exhibiting leadership qualities. By focusing on the vision of an organization, its values, and its relationship to the operational units and the community, individuals can lead a discussion, a project, a business unit, or even a university. Developing and honing leadership skills can serve you well in both university and personal life.

Local user groups, conference program committees, ad hoc working groups, and advisory groups abound with opportunities for you to take on leadership roles. Many of these groups are member-driven and highly participatory, and they rely on volunteers to get things done. Offer to chair a small working group—this is usually a greatly appreciated first step toward taking on larger roles. Often these chair positions simply require that you keep the group on track, coordinate meetings, and provide summary reports of the group's work to the sponsoring association or society. You may find yourself facilitating communication, resolving conflict, and developing strategy as well. These roles also give you the opportunity to influence the work's direction, so if you feel passionate about an issue, you are in a position to have your ideas heard.

Navigating Professional Associations and Societies

A quick look at the Pocket Guide to U.S. Higher Education 2005 <http://www.educause.edu/LibraryDetailPage/666?ID=PUB2201> *shows more than 3,700 institutions of higher education in the United States and over 15 million students. Many societies, associations, and professional groups support this population. The* Pocket Guide *contains a listing of relevant associations and organizations, beginning on page 49.*

Professional associations serve the community by:

▶ *Providing opportunities for professional development and mentoring*
▶ *Serving as a place for creating the profession and fostering innovation*
▶ *Nurturing a sense of community*
▶ *Advocating for the interests of higher education*
▶ *Facilitating information exchange and information development*

Of the associations and societies with which IT professionals typically interact, some are academic societies, created around a specific discipline, like the Society for Information Management (SIM) or the Association for Computing Machinery (ACM). Others reflect the interests of particular types of institutions, such as the Council of Independent Colleges (CIC) or the American Association of Community Colleges (AACC), and still others were formed around a profession, like the National Association of College and University Attorneys (NACUA), the American Library Association (ALA), EDUCAUSE, or the National Association of College and University Business Officers (NACUBO). Most have regular publications, host Web sites with libraries of information, hold annual and/or regional conferences, and offer other professional development events and opportunities, both online and in person.

Enhance Communication Skills

Calvin: *Sometimes when I'm talking, my words can't keep up with my thoughts. I wonder why we think faster than we speak.*

Hobbes: *Probably so we can think twice.* — *Calvin & Hobbes*, Bill Watterson

Most if not all of our campus IT positions these days list "good communications skills" as a job requirement. The ability to listen well and to speak and write clearly becomes increasingly important, even critical, moving through the different stages of a career. As levels of job responsibility increase, so does the requirement for addressing project teams, committees, boards, visitors, faculty, staff, and students. Just about everyone who works in IT today must be able to clearly translate techie jargon into understandable terms for the campus community.

Answering a call for proposals for a conference or workshop lets you formally share your work while building your writing and public speaking skills. Most of us remember that first presentation, and many experienced speakers still get "butterflies" when stepping up to the podium, but it gets easier with practice. Similarly, writing an article for a Web or print journal gives you the experience of working with an editor and/or a committee of reviewers. While not everyone in our community faces the requirement to publish, many societies and associations offer the opportunity to gain exposure and to contribute to the body of knowledge through formal publication processes. In addition to writing articles for journals, many of which are peer reviewed, you can maintain a timely and topical blog, write chapters for books, or contribute to a white paper or position paper.

Find Career Opportunities

Destiny is not a matter of chance. It is a matter of choice: it is not to be waited for, it is a thing to be achieved. —William Jennings Bryan

Where will you find your next job? Most people do not make their job connections through the want ads or the *Chronicle* job listings, although they are useful sources of information. Maintaining a level of professional activity not only provides some short-term benefits, it can—and should—become part of your long-term career plan. By being active in the profession, you make lifelong contacts and establish your name in the community. The same colleagues you consult for assistance on a problem can offer good career advice. The person you met at a conference or through a working group last year might well contact you about a job next year. It happens all the time.

Change Your Environment

A desk is a dangerous place from which to view the world. —John Le Carré

Sometimes it can be incredibly useful to leave campus—a day or two at a professional event, whether a conference, a workshop, or a training program often provides additional time for reflection and renewal. Many of us find a change of environment, away from the day-to-day pressures of campus IT, rejuvenating. If the event you attend is stimulating, you will return with new ideas to share and discuss with your colleagues. Evenings and breaks offer time not only for networking but also for personal planning. Organizing your thoughts, thinking strategically about your unit—even making career plans seems easier when you are out of the office.

External engagement brings with it some challenges, too, not the least of which is being away from family. Overcommitting yourself can lead to difficulties both at home and on campus, so managing time well is critical. Finally, others on your campus might suspect that your priorities do not lie with the institution if you are involved in professional activities. You can mitigate this perception by educating colleagues about the nature of your professional activities and helping them understand the benefits to the campus from your involvement.

Make Friends and Have Fun

We know what we are, but know not what we may be. —Shakespeare

While the rewards of professional involvement manifest in better access to resources, lifelong learning opportunities, skill development, and career enhancement, some of the more gratifying aspects of active participation in the profession are the personal connections you make and the sense of community that develops through interaction with your peers. Our community has developed a series of awards and recognitions to honor those among us who have made exemplary contributions to the profession, and we gather periodically within various groups such as the Association for Computing Machinery (ACM, <http://www.acm.org/>), EDUCAUSE, or the Coalition for Networked Information (CNI) to bestow those awards with great pleasure. For many of us, though, it is the personal friendships that develop through our common interests in higher education and in technology that add rewarding dimensions to our professional lives.

Next Steps

If you want to participate more broadly in the profession, and you are convinced that this engagement should be part of your own professional development plan, what steps should you take?

Understanding some of the venues for professional participation is important. For those of us working in higher education, opportunities to get involved are numerous. They exist on our own campuses, in the region, and with national and international professional societies and associations. Table 1 summarizes some of the places you can look and the ways you can participate. Local, state, and regional entities, or even chapters of larger associations, typically offer lower travel costs—which translates into lower barriers to entry—than do their national or international counterparts. Keep in mind that there is value to broadening participation beyond IT to include other campus perspectives, including business officers, librarians, planning officers, and institutional researchers. Looking at IT groups outside higher education is important, too—investigate local or national technology associations like the Society for Information Management (SIM) or your city's technology council. Use your existing network of colleagues to introduce you to relevant opportunities, and ask people to recommend you for assignments in professional activities.

Table 1. Opportunities for Professional Engagement

Venue	Initial Engagement	Greater Involvement	Leadership Activity
Publications	Read	Contribute	Serve on editorial board
Electronic forums (listservs, blogs, mailing lists)	Read	Contribute/post	Moderate
Conferences	Attend	Present	Serve on program committee
Seminars	Attend	Present	Organize
Task forces, committees, and working groups	Read and use reports	Participate	Lead
Professional associations and organizations	Leadership roles	Serve on board	Serve as officer
Community engagement	Visit other campuses	Host visits to your campus	Host larger events
Community service	Serve on visiting committees	Serve as a consultant	Serve on and/or lead accreditation teams

By getting involved—presenting your work, writing for the profession, or volunteering to serve on committees, working groups, or boards—you will not only build a network and grow professionally but also have rewarding experiences and make connections that will last a lifetime.

About the Authors

Cynthia Golden is a vice president of EDUCAUSE. Her responsibilities include many facets of professional development, from conferences and seminars to Web content to print. She previously held IT management and leadership positions at Carnegie Mellon University, MIT, and Duquesne University.

Dan Updegrove served for more than a decade on the staff of Educom (predecessor to EDUCAUSE), held IT management positions at the University of Pennsylvania and Yale University, and now is vice president for IT and CIO at The University of Texas at Austin. He recently played a key role in founding LEARN, the Lonestar Education and Research Network.

CHAPTER 7

Work and Life: Achieving a Reasonable Balance

Tracey Leger-Hornby
Brandeis University

Ron Bleed
Maricopa Community College District

"Can I really do this job well and have a life?" If you've found yourself asking that question, you're not alone. It is not unusual to hear IT staff say they feel they have too much to do and not enough time. In a world with expectations of service 24 hours a day, seven days a week, IT staff often feel pressure to put in long hours, to work from home, and to be constantly on call, online, and available. At times of great stress—or at annual performance review time—this question of balancing work and home life is bound to come up. Contemplating a new job where the levels of responsibility will increase also raises the issue.

Studies show that IT workers have more difficulty with work/life balance than their non-IT counterparts do.[1] In casual conversations with colleagues both on our own campuses and around the country, we often hear people express the feeling that they have not achieved what they consider an acceptable balance between work and personal interests. The research supports these perceptions. Working long hours, working on the weekends, and bringing work home are most often noted as the major disrupters to work/life balance.[2] Many studies, including a summary in *Communications of the ACM*,[3] have also pointed to the perceived variability in the work/life balance depending on gender, generation, culture, income level, and type of job.

The problem is also affecting the pipeline of potential IT leaders. A 2004 ECAR study of the IT profession in higher education found that the typical IT professional is a male over 40 who works more than 50 hours per week.[4] It also reports a lack of interest among respondents—particularly women in mid-management positions—in advancing to the senior-most IT positions. Another study found this phenomenon in the wider population as well.[5] This study showed a trend among both women and men that involves lowering career ambitions to avoid having to make the personal trade-offs associated with advancing to jobs having more responsibility. While a number of factors might influence decisions not to pursue more senior-level IT positions, it is difficult to discount the perception—or reality—that senior IT jobs are just too demanding. All our employees have to do is look around to see the long hours that their managers and leaders work.

A growing trend in today's workforce puts a greater emphasis on living a successful, happy life versus simply achieving success at work.[6] A recent study found that employees who place a similar priority on family life and work ("dual-centric" people) had advanced more in their careers than those who are "work-centric" or "family-centric." Dual-centric and family-centric employees also exhibited a greater satisfaction with their jobs and lives than work-centric employees.

Does trying to balance work and personal life have to cause problems, conflicts, guilt, and tensions both at work and at home? We believe this balancing act can be done successfully, to the benefit of both job and family. Commitments to family, church, community groups, and others make our lives rich and rewarding. Performing well in a challenging position, at an interesting place with friendly colleagues also brings satisfaction. The pressure to do it all and do it well is strong in our society. Finding ways to bring a sense of balance to your life—to feel successful in your job and happy in your outside activities, is what we address in this chapter, suggesting strategies for both the supervisor and the employee and making a call to action for the IT leadership at higher education institutions.

Personal Values—What Drives You?

Whether or not you realize it, the decisions you make are influenced by what you value—the beliefs, attitudes, and ideas you think are important. These values shape the choices all of us make in our lives, and understanding more about them helps us make choices we can live with, both for our careers and our personal lives. Identifying and understanding your own values is a first step toward understanding your current position and helping you make adjustments to achieve the balance you desire.

Numerous values assessment tools are available in books, in journal articles, and on career development Web sites. Several university career counseling centers, including Arizona State University (http://career.asu.edu/S/careerplan/selfdiscovery/ValuesAssessment.htm) and the University of British Columbia (http://www.sauder.ubc.ca/ccc/docs/AssessmentHandouts.pdf), can get you thinking about what is important to you. Start by examining the *intrinsic* values, or the things that provide you with inner satisfaction, such as working for a good cause or experiencing adventure, and the *extrinsic* values, such as your salary, job title, or level of authority at work. Factor in lifestyle values, too, such as living in a rural or urban setting, having time for spiritual or personal growth, spending time with family, or being active in your community.

Evaluating the Gap

Looking at the values you have identified as most important to you and then reflecting on how you spend your time, do you see any gaps? How have the values you ranked most important influenced your career choices and your life choices? Might you need to make changes to bring your work or your personal life more in line with what you value? Prioritize the multiple roles you perform so that you make decisions and set limits between the demands of work and your home life. To focus, organize your life priorities.

Managing Priorities

You can take two simple yet important steps to limit the demands of work and manage priorities. Understanding the job and knowing the schedule can clarify and simplify the overwhelming list of things to do. The suggestions that follow are divided into two sections, for an employee and for a supervisor. Looking at both may give you insight into the workplace environment and the work/life balance.

Understanding the Job—for Employees

▶ **Develop a broad perspective.** Understanding how higher education works can help you decide if you want to stay in the field. Working in higher education is not the same as going to college or attending graduate school. For IT, higher education may be as pressured an environment as any corporation. Getting summers off in higher education is a myth for IT—summer is the busy season for many IT departments trying to catch up on systems upgrades while students and faculty are not on campus. At the same time, summer may be the most difficult season for parents of young children who need to balance summer camps, vacation, and simple relaxation with hectic, high-pressure schedules at work.

▶ **Know the goals.** For a staff member, knowing why something must be done can be very helpful. A good deal of frustration from having too much on your plate can be relieved by understanding the project goals. It is also easier to discuss how to balance workload if you have the whole picture.

- **Understand expectations.** Make sure you understand your job description and the expectations of your supervisors. For example, a frequent point of contention is after-hours communications. Are staff members expected to check e-mail in the evenings or on weekends? Do you have to carry a cell phone or a pager? What are the policies covering off-hours? If you take responsibility for meeting communications expectations, you should be able to take time off without guilt or recrimination.

Understanding the Job—for Supervisors

- **Know the goals.** Really understanding the environment and expectations of your job makes setting priorities simpler. Maintaining perspective on what is important—what must be done immediately and what can wait—becomes easier if you see the big picture. A supervisor must determine and communicate goals and objectives clearly. Know where you are going and what you expect yourself and others to do. Be available for questions, and anticipate them. Explain how your department fits into the larger environment. Describe the issues and options. Do not expect everyone to understand your perspective every time. Be patient.

- **Distribute decision making.** One way to help staff understand priorities is to let staff work with you in setting them. If you can, bring the issues to the table and present the full picture. What resources are available? Are there constraints or issues to address? What are the deadlines? Can the work be distributed across departments? After an open and creative discussion, new alternatives to accomplishing goals may arise, and the team feels a sense of engagement from going through the process together.

- **Set clear expectations.** Clearly communicate expectations around work schedules. If you work 50 hours a week, do you expect everyone to do that? If you arrive at 8:00 a.m., should everyone be there? Is flextime an option? Do departmental habits or customs dictate staff hours? Can staff telecommute regularly? Do they have Internet access at home provided as part of their compensation packages? What about laptops? Decide on acceptable behaviors and be explicit about your expectations. What are the policies? You can take the following specific steps to achieve clarity:
  - Work with staff and human resources to develop a set of operational norms that include work hours. Communicate these to everyone.
  - If people do not meet expectations (for example, by coming in at 10:00 a.m.

each day), let them know immediately. Tell them what you expect (everyone at their desks by 9:00 a.m.) and ask for the rationale behind the later arrival time. Perhaps the expectations were not clear, or the person might have a long commute or childcare responsibilities. If exceptions are not acceptable, you will need to work out a performance plan to ensure changes.

▶ Publish clear policies on after-hours coverage. If you expect staff to check e-mail at regular intervals on weekends, make it part of the job description and orientation. Do not assume everyone knows what he or she should do.

Know the Schedule—for Employees

▶ **Understand business cycles.** If you know that the end of August and early September will be busy on campus, try not to plan competing events at home. This is not always possible, of course, especially if you have young children starting school who need extra time to adjust. Discuss options for a more flexible schedule with your supervisor—in advance.

▶ **Share the load.** Get to know your colleagues. If you build good relationships with them, it will be easier to spot areas of overlap. Know the team's strengths and weaknesses, and share the burdens. If you see another team member struggling with something, offer to assist. Then when you are under pressure, chances are co-workers will help you in return.

▶ **Communicate often.** Communication is key. For supervisors, employees, and communities, it is important to keep communication flowing. Understand the relevant goals, know the priorities and who has responsibility for each task, and be clear on the deadlines. Share questions and concerns before problems get out of hand. Maintaining good communication with partners at home is also critical. Further, knowing when problems really are based at work and not at home can help prevent arguments. It is also important to keep a sense of humor and perspective.

Know the Schedule—for Supervisors

▶ **Know cycles and patterns.** Higher education has routine events and regular cycles. Every year the academic calendar dictates the work on a college or university campus. Developing a calendar of activities and reviewing it with the staff well in advance of the events is basic to good project planning and can help avoid surprises and late nights at work.

▶ **Accommodate the schedule.** The back-to-school time can be particularly taxing and affect schedules more than other times of the year. Hiring temporary workers and scheduling student workers for fall hours *before* they leave for the summer break are two useful techniques. Working across traditional boundaries can also be helpful. For example, the administrative systems group is busy at the end of the fiscal year, not at the start of the fall semester, so some staff time may be available to assist with fall activities. At Brandeis, everyone in the Library and Technology Services division pitches in on Opening Sunday, when new students arrive. A tremendous team-building event that provides great visibility for the department, it also provides help to the small group supporting student computing and telephony when they need it most.

Productivity and Managing Time

Controlling the demands of work and being productive requires that you manage your time well. This is easier said than done, but a few basics will help you find the model that works best for you.

Managing Time—for Employees

▶ **Create a schedule.** Follow a schedule as much as possible. If your work offers a shared calendar utility, use it—it's easier to schedule meetings and make effective use of everyone's time. If you can keep to a routine schedule and mark blocks of time for regular tasks, you can better plan and execute your work. Once you get into a routine, you will see how long it actually takes to do something and become better at predicting your schedule.

▶ **Find a time-management strategy.** Many time management models can help you organize your schedule. David Allen proposed one popular approach, chiefly making and using lists. Allen's model offers ways to collect things that demand attention, process them, organize the results, review options, and do something about them. His theory is, do it now or do it later, and schedule it, delegate it, or forget it.[7]

▶ **Plan some uninterrupted time.** Reserve an hour of quiet time every day, and close your office door if you can. Use the uninterrupted time to catch up on e-mail, work on projects, or return calls. Marking that hour a day in your calendar will keep others in the department from scheduling you then. If taking that time during the day is not possible, try to schedule it at the end or beginning of the day. Know the flow of work around you, and adjust to it.

Managing Time—for Supervisors

▶ **Respect others.** Your calendar is important, yes, but remember to respect your staff's time as well. Hold meetings only when necessary, and keep them short. Check to see if staff are busy before initiating a meeting. Give advance warning on the time and topic. All meetings should have agendas and minutes.

▶ **Open door policy.** If you need time to concentrate on writing or making calls, put the time into your calendar and shut the door. As long as others know the signal, and you are available for consultation on a regular basis, holding aside occasional periods of solitude will not cause a problem.

When Worlds Collide

Making choices is what the balance between work and life is all about. There may be times when the choice between moving ahead with your career takes a back seat to your health or happiness at home. How to make choices and deal with the demands for your time and energy are up to you. The values you identify as important can guide you in making decisions.

One of the places where conflict arises, for women in particular, comes during childbearing years. The decisions on having children, whether to interrupt career plans, how soon to return to work, and how to manage ongoing child care are a source of conflict for many workers. According to a 2002 RAND study, whether women remain in the workforce

> will depend to a great extent on working parents' ability to balance work and family. As a woman enters the labor force, not all of her homemaker responsibilities will be transferred to others. These dual work and homemaker responsibilities can strain a woman's limits on time and effort. Women (and their spouses or partners who share in homemaking responsibilities) are therefore likely to increasingly favor family-friendly workplace policies and benefits.[8]

Similarly, working adults may face greater demands when it comes to caring for aging parents. According to the same RAND study, the proportion of elderly people requiring help with daily activities increased from 35 percent in 1984 to nearly 43 percent in 2004.[9] To provide this help, middle-aged and older workers may increasingly need flexible scheduling and assistance with finding caregivers. Individuals who care for both children and aging parents may feel pressure from both sides at the same time.

Fortunately for many of us, institutions of higher education have led the way in providing policies and services that support faculty and staff. On-campus child care, health and wellness programs, telecommuting opportunities, flexible working hours, and more generous leave policies can assist staff in balancing these family and work demands. Careful, thoughtful, and open communication with your supervisor, your colleagues, your partner, and your family is critical to dealing with these special demands.

Dealing with Burnout

We have all heard colleagues describe themselves as having had enough of the pressures and demands of the job. Not only do self-described workaholics experience high levels of stress and anxiety, but even those who try hard to maintain a reasonable work/life balance will at times succumb to stress. Burnout is not simply excessive stress but a complex reaction to ongoing stress—"a physical, mental, and emotional response" that often includes emotional exhaustion and an increasingly negative attitude toward work and perhaps life.[10] A person who is overwhelmed, overworked, or burned out can not only be ineffective in his or her job and have a very negative effect on colleagues but also is at risk of serious depression that can threaten employment, relationships, and health. College and university health centers and counseling centers have resources available to help individuals deal with job burnout and identify early indicators of a developing problem. It is important for all of us to observe the early signs of burnout and develop strategies to avoid it.

Mental health associations, counseling centers, and career Web sites offer lots of advice on how to identify problems and monitor levels of stress. Not surprisingly, many of the strategies for preventing burnout are the same as those recommended for managing stress. A good tool for understanding and preventing burnout is available from coping.org (http://www.coping.org/growth/burnout.htm). Examining and making changes to your job or even to your daily routine can help prevent stress from building.

Making Changes

This may seem dramatic, but many times a drastic change is needed to obtain your desired balance. If your work schedule is excessive or inflexible, seek remedies from your institution—talk candidly about the situation with your supervisor. Flexible scheduling tends to increase employee satisfaction and lessen the conflict between work and family. When the work schedule fits poorly with an employee's preferences, burnout is more likely.

If your institution cannot accommodate you, you may want to seek other positions at other places. IT is a very mobile profession; use that to your advantage. If IT is the source of your problems with balance, consider changing careers. For some people, the fast pace of change in technology may be a reason to get off the IT career track.

Strategies to Promote Balance—for Employees

▶ **Take time off.** Work has been hectic for months and things at home have been busy. Tension has been building for weeks. What should you do? Plan a vacation and take it! Your vacation can be a day on the porch with a good book, a picnic by a river or lake with the kids, or a trip to a far away location. The point is—it is not work. A break in the routine, even a small one, can bring back perspective. Relaxation is important for good physical and mental health.

▶ **Take a lunch break.** This may not always be possible, but no one should work through lunch every day. Get outside into the fresh air and sunshine. Take a 10-minute walk. Take care of yourself, and then you can take care of others.

▶ **Exercise.** Working up a good sweat eliminates lots of frustration and has many other benefits. It takes time to make the commitment, so work on managing your calendar and your time. Make exercise a priority.

▶ **Volunteer.** Join a committee and get a new perspective on the organization. Meet new people and give yourself a new challenge. Volunteering can lead to a new job, help you contribute to your organization or community, and break up your routine.

▶ **Learn something new.** Teach a class or take one. Can you use the class to make your job easier? Or to help you get another job in the future?

▶ **Laugh.** Keep your sense of humor. Read the comics every day. Tell a silly joke. Blow bubbles.

▶ **Get help.** Ask for help if you need it.

Strategies to Promote Balance—for Supervisors

▶ **Be a role model.** Follow the preceding advice and let your employees do the same. Work on making your organization healthy and productive. No one is irreplaceable, and no one needs to be there all the time. You may find your employees more relaxed when you have been away—they can get things done in your absence. Insist that staff take all the vacation they earn. One IT division at an institution in the east implemented a policy where every IT staff member was required to take five consecutive working days of vacation every year. Temporary staff can help if necessary. Train other people to help where they can—cross-training is a morale builder that benefits everyone in the organization. Remember that you are a role model for your employees. What kind of manager or leader do they see? Can you find positive ways to change your behavior? It will help them as well.

▶ **Cultivate the next generation.** Build a good team with good managers and next-generation leaders. If you have a good team working for you, you can relax more yourself. The trust you have in each other will provide the stability and structure needed for letting people take vacation or pass tasks to team members.

▶ **Promote camaraderie.** Allow for humor and play in the organization. Food is a great icebreaker and a way to get people to mingle. Could you have lunch as a group? Are there playing fields nearby for a quick softball game? How about bowling during a winter break? Movies and popcorn? Potluck lunches? Do you do team-building exercises during meetings to get to know each other? Do you have casual dress days? Do you have "team" shirts or other types of rewards for staff? Anything outside the routine can help in creating a strong team, but remember to respect individual preferences on participation.

▶ **Use your resources.** Use your human resources department as a place to get advice when staff members need help. Often the HR office can point to resources or offer suggestions on how to open up channels of communication.

Conclusion

Our profession is full of people who have found ways to achieve a balance that works for them, providing career satisfaction and personal fulfillment. It can be done. Finding that balance is key. We believe that IT professionals who build supportive, friendly relationships with their co-workers and network with their higher education counterparts feel more satisfied with their jobs and more able to achieve a work/life balance.

While this chapter provides advice and techniques for finding and maintaining a healthy work/life balance, our work leads us to conclude also that as a profession we must make a concerted effort to pay attention to the jobs that we ask people to do. We in leadership roles need to carefully manage the job expectations and requirements so that requirements are realistic and expectations can be met without excessive compromises. Clearly, doing so is in the best interests of our institutions and our employees.

Endnotes

1. "IT Careers and Work Life Balance," *CIO Online Magazine* (September 17, 2001), <http://www2.cio.com/research/surveyreport.cfm?id=18>.

2. Ibid.

3. Thomas Schambach and J. Ellis Blanton, "The Professional Development Challenge for IT Professionals," *Communications of the ACM*, vol. 45, no. 4 (April 2002), pp. 83–87. For another example of similar research, see Gina Hernez-Broome and Richard J. Hughes, "Leadership Development: Past, Present, and Future," *Human Resource Planning*, vol. 27, no. 1 (2004), pp. 24–32.

4. Richard N. Katz et al., *Information Technology Leadership in Higher Education: The Condition of the Community* (Boulder, Colo.: EDUCAUSE Center for Applied Research, research study, vol. 1, 2004), p. 13, <http://www.educause.edu/LibraryDetailPage/666?ID=ERS0401>.

5. American Business Collaborative, "Generation and Gender in the Workplace: An Issue Brief by Families and Work Institute" (Boston: American Business Collaborative, October 2004), <http://familiesandwork.org/eproducts/genandgender.pdf>.

6. Ibid.

7. David Allen, *Getting Things Done: The Art of Stress-Free Productivity* (New York: Penguin Books, 2001). His Web site (http://www.davidco.com/what_is_gtd.php) describes his methodology and offers suggestions to get started. Allen also made the point that everything we do, both work and personal tasks, should be viewed together. On any given day you may have to write project specifications, take your daughter to basketball practice, attend a meeting with the provost, and pay your property taxes. He argued that his methods, in order to be effective, need to apply across the work/life spectrum. This translates into keeping all of your tasks on one calendar.

8. Lynn A. Karoly and Constantijn W. A. Panis, *The 21st Century at Work: Forces Shaping the Future Workforce and Workplace in the United States* (Santa Monica, Calif.: RAND Corporation, 2004), <http://www.rand.org/pubs/monographs/2004/RAND_MG164.pdf>.

9. Ibid.

10. Sheila Hutman et al., "Burnout: Signs, Symptoms, and Prevention," helpguide.org, <http://www.helpguide.org/mental/burnout_signs_symptoms.htm#what>.

Useful Web References

Work/Life Balance

▶ Articles with strategies for overcoming burnout: <http://www.inc.com/guides/growth/20792.html>

▶ A collection of articles on work/life balance: <http://www.fastcompany.com/articles_by_topic/balance>

▶ New Zealand Project on Work Life Balance: <http://www.dol.govt.nz/worklife/index.asp>

▶ Institute on Work & Family at Boston College: <http://www.bc.edu/centers/cwf/research/>

Ways to Work

▶ David Allen: <http://www.davidco.com/>

▶ Publications on appreciative inquiry and thinking differently about how we work: <http://appreciativeinquiry.cwru.edu/research/bibPublished.cfm>

▶ Marcus Buckingham, author and keynote speaker at EDUCAUSE 2004, about thinking positively about how we work: <http://www.marcusbuckingham.com/>

▶ Seven Habits of Highly Effective People: <http://www.franklincovey.com/foryou/articles/seven.html>

Women in Technology

▶ A collection of articles on women in leadership: <http://www.fastcompany.com/guides/leadwoman.html>

▶ Listserv and forum for women in technology: <http://www.systers.org/>

▶ American Association of University Women: <http://www.aauw.org/>; see especially <http://www.aauw.org/research/womenatwork.cfm>

▶ Women in Technology International: <http://www.witi.org/>

▶ University of Massachusetts at Lowell site on Women at Work, with references to other resources: <http://www.uml.edu/centers/women-work/>

▶ Professional development and networking for women in technical professions: <http://www.womenintechnology.org/>

▶ The Anita Borg Institute: <http://www.anitaborg.org/>

▶ The National Center for Women & Information Technology: <http://www.ncwit.org/>

About the Authors

Tracey Leger-Hornby is associate CIO at Brandeis University, where she develops strategic initiatives for the Library and Technology Services division. Leger-Hornby received her PhD in higher education administration from Boston College, her master's of library service degree from Dalhousie University in Halifax, Nova Scotia, and her BA in psychology and education from Simmons College. She has served on the board of trustees of the New England Computer Program (NERCOMP) since 1994 and has held the offices of chair, treasurer, and secretary.

Ron Bleed is vice chancellor emeritus of the Maricopa Community College District. He was vice chancellor for information technologies at the Maricopa Community Colleges until his retirement at the end of 2005 and held CIO-level positions in higher education for 39 years, with the past 25 at Maricopa. He served as chair of the EDUCAUSE Board for two years, and in 2005 received the EDUCAUSE Excellence in Leadership Award at the EDUCAUSE National Conference.

CHAPTER 8

12 Habits of Successful IT Professionals

Brian L. Hawkins
EDUCAUSE

This chapter was first published in EDUCAUSE Review, *vol. 41, no. 1 (January/ February 2006), pp. 56–67,* <http://www.educause.edu/LibraryDetailPage/ 666?ID=ERM0613>.

In all positions, professionals must continue to develop their skills. The higher ed IT profession is no exception. However, many of these skills should be developed progressively. If IT professionals can start learning these skills early in their careers, they will have a good chance of turning the skills into habits—and of becoming successful and effective IT professionals. Below I have identified 12 such habits, involving objectives or skills that I feel are key to the success of IT professionals.[1]

1. They Are Multilingual
Many years ago, I was interviewing for a CIO position at Brown University. Howard Swearer, the president of Brown at that time, asked me, "What is the greatest strength that you would bring to the position?" I contemplated for a moment and answered, "I am multilingual." He stared at me for a moment, as if I had lost my mind entirely. I proceeded to explain that I was capable of effectively communicating with faculty, with students, with vendors, with trustees, and with other administrators. I was not trying to be flippant: the CIO needs to be able to interact effectively and be respected by a variety of quite disparate audiences.

Effectiveness of interaction, especially on campus, is based on whether an individual can understand the concerns and problems being faced by a particular user, as well as that user's professional dilemmas. This is true on the academic side of the house, where one needs to understand the technology requirements and problems of a particle physicist, a classicist, or an economist. There are different needs for data files, transmission speeds, and many other IT issues that directly affect the scholarship of these varying disciplines. The ability to understand some of these scholarly requirements is essential to being perceived as a partner in the academic enterprise rather than just as some bureaucrat who has responsibility for the IT environment on campus.

The same is true on the administrative side of the house. If the IT professional has some working knowledge of the challenges facing financial aid, the auditor, or the admissions office, the sense of "being in this together" increases substantially. The problem is that gaining this working knowledge takes time—time spent listening to users and reading and following key issues in the *Chronicle of Higher Education* or other news sources—in order to become and then stay informed on current challenges. Trying to become an expert in all of these areas is completely unrealistic, but showing an interest in coming up to some basic speed on key issues and concerns provides an entrée that can set the stage for the IT professional—and the technology organization that he or she represents—to be perceived as a partner in the larger enterprise.

2. They Avoid the Unconscious Conspiracy

In the absolutely terrific book *Why Leaders Can't Lead: The Unconscious Conspiracy Continues*, Warren Bennis explained that leaders are impaired—if not prevented—in leading because they become consumed by the routine. He suggested that individuals with the full capability to lead their organizations often fail because they drown in the tidal waves of minutia, mundane details, and dailiness associated with their jobs, which take all of their time and energy. There is not adequate time left to think about the bigger issues, to do the necessary visioning for their organizations, and to look over the horizon. All of us have certainly felt that our jobs are a bit overwhelming, but if we succumb to these pressures and daily issues, and fail to do this thinking about the longer term and the strategic issues, we will fail as leaders and as IT professionals. So, how do we find the time and prioritize in a fashion that allows us to keep the "unconscious conspiracy" at bay?

Bennis provided a number of strategies for doing this, including designating the time to do this broader thinking. That means blocking time on the calendar and not just grabbing time when it presents itself. For me, this time is early in the morning, when nobody is around to drop in the office, when nobody calls on the phone, and when I am fresh and rested. Others will find their own times and rhythms for such thinking, but one thing is clear: it needs to be blocked time; if it's not, other tasks will soak up all the available time.

Bennis also suggested interacting with people other than your closest professional colleagues, or what he refers to as the "palace guard": those who may often think like you do, who may want to please you, and who may have a vested interest in things staying the way they are. This too necessitates time—time to have coffee or lunch or just to visit with members of various campus committees, with staff in administrative offices, and with faculty critics. But these discussions can yield different and potentially new perspectives, as well as increasing your knowledge of other areas.

3. They Read Broadly

Perhaps the most important strategy that Bennis suggested for leaders is to change their reading habits. What leaders read in many ways shapes their views on issues, and although reading also takes time, it is essential to understanding what is routine and what is strategic and to developing a broader view of the environmental factors that are affecting the technology, the campus, and higher education as a whole.

In many ways, the things people read define their worldview and the reality they use to define their professional strategies and directions. A person who aspires to a higher position or to a more responsible position needs to have a broader understanding of higher education, technology, and best practices in a variety of information resource arenas. Some suggestions are to find out what other higher education leaders are reading, review the new books in the *Chronicle* listing, and see what is new and relevant in periodicals such as *Harvard Business Review*, *Change*, *Business Officer*, and of course *EDUCAUSE Review*.

Keeping up-to-date with happenings in higher education means reading most if not all of the major sections of the *Chronicle*, not just the section or the articles in a specific professional area. To achieve the breadth needed for a successful IT career, one should have at least an awareness, if not a working understanding, of all areas in the college or university—including financial aid, athletics, and international concerns. Only by having this awareness can an IT professional more fully appreciate the myriad pressures that the senior administration is trying to balance, as well as those areas in which new technologies or approaches may assist the campus more broadly. A variety of electronic digests also cover key breaking stories and challenges and can be an easy way to keep in touch with the complexities of campus life and scholarship. In addition, reading the letters to the editor or participating (or simply lurking) on listservs or blogs about higher education issues can greatly assist in understanding higher ed issues.

Finally, a word about career planning is in order. Even if you are not currently looking for a new position, it is worthwhile to explore the relevant job postings in the *Chronicle* or on the EDUCAUSE Web site. Understanding the job requirements (and also the changing nature of these requirements) provides a better idea of what search committees are looking for in given positions. By reading these, employees are not being disloyal to their institution but are trying to get a better understanding of areas in which to grow and develop. Similarly, reading the "Gazette" section of the *Chronicle* reveals patterns of where people are moving from and to, leading to a better understanding of the boundaries that are capable of being crossed and of how career mobility is working in today's environment.

4. They Educate Others About Information-Based Organizations

IT professionals need to actively help others understand the ways that the new technologies and new information flows are affecting the very essence of the college or university. This applies especially to the process of educating senior institutional officers. Today's institutional leaders need to know that they are responsible for more than the financial and human resources. They also are responsible for the information resources under their control. This is a relatively new phenomenon, and it is one that needs to be embraced by all senior officers. The enterprise systems that so many campuses have implemented are beginning to redefine information assets, in that particular information is no longer considered (or at least should not be considered) "the registrar's information" or the "admission director's information." Instead, such information should be looked on as the institution's information.

Thinking of information as an institutional asset is critical to effectively managing today's complex institutions of higher education; however, all too often, the senior institutional officers would like to keep the issues of technology and information off of their desks and to relegate these issues to the CIO or to other specialized professionals. To quote from an earlier article:

> On most campuses, a significant amount of continuing education needs to be provided so that the entire senior team can assume these new responsibilities. The CIO must be integrally involved in shaping this education, but ultimately the campus strategy and the commitment of the executive team to work collaboratively will be critical. Although higher education has historically been organized in vertical

administrative structures, technology is a cross-cutting function, creating horizontal interdependencies that require administrators to manage these campus-wide functions. This interdependent and nonhierarchical characteristic of information technology implies that campus leadership teams need to develop competencies within their own functional areas and need to work jointly in defining the strategic value of IT investments—in short, defining information technology in terms of its instrumentality rather than as a cost center.[2]

Institutional leaders must understand that our colleges and universities are information-based organizations, that technology facilitates highly interdependent relationships between organizational units, and that the traditional stovepiped or vertical structures are inadequate to manage the information-based institution. This educational responsibility is an obligation that all IT professionals need to actively assume.

5. They Understand the Limits of Their Advocacy

Effective IT professionals need to make clear their understanding that the college or university has other priorities with which it must deal. Others at the decision-making table need to know that the IT professional has an appreciation for and understanding of some of their problems and issues. In trying to advance particular goals, the IT professional should consider reducing their importance if other campus needs take precedence. In the management concept known as *suboptimization*, a given unit of an organization advances as premier in an organization that is not fully achieving its overall goals. For example, an automobile manufacturer that has the best research and development unit in the world but that has marginal sales and marketing and is therefore failing economically is experiencing suboptimization. Maximizing a subunit at the expense of the institution is improper and foolhardy. In advancing a given IT effort or other initiative, the IT professional must do so fully in support of the primary goals and objectives of the institution and not just to advance the IT unit for its own sake.

Many in the campus community already perceive IT as a black hole that will potentially absorb all of the resources of the college or university. Careful thought must be given to each initiative and to how each can advance the mission of the institution. Then, and only then, will such efforts gain the institutional support that is essential. To appear to be (or, worse yet, to actually be) selfish in looking for resources from the institution is perhaps the quickest way to lose campus credibility. Certainly, one needs to be thorough and up-front about the resources that are necessary to advance a given project, but all proposals must be cast within the parameters of institutional goals. Discussing and building support for this goal of alignment is a critical part of being an effective IT leader.

6. They Are Cautious When Speaking Publicly

With the increasing dependency of colleges and universities on information technology and on accessing information electronically, there is often public interest in what campuses are doing with this technology and information. There also is a downside to this public interest. When campuses experience security failures or when confidential information has been exposed, IT professionals are called on to speak to reporters and other officials. These are often ticklish situations. Although most IT professionals have not been trained in this arena, it is often thrust upon them, and they need to be cautious that using part of their "fifteen minutes of fame" does not result in infamy.

If possible, the IT professional should tell immediate superiors and possibly other senior officers that he or she is being asked to speak to the press on a given issue, since the senior leaders may prefer to have someone else handle such matters. Sometimes this advance notice is impossible, of course. If caught in the position of making public statements, the IT professional should make sure these other campus officers know immediately. If sensitive information is involved and the reporter does not honor a request to go off the record, the IT professional needs to know which information can go public and should be careful not to volunteer too much information, especially if the issue involves a sensitive or potentially embarrassing circumstance for the institution.

Certainly, not all encounters with the press are highly volatile situations, but reporters are often looking to make a story rather than to educate the community. IT professionals need to proceed cautiously and should remember not to use too much jargon. The reporters probably do not know even the basics about technology, nor will they have done all that much homework on a topic. The IT professional needs to identify key highlights and principles and not make too many clarifications or get too detailed, even if the simplistic version isn't 100 percent accurate technically. Reporters can be referred to particular policies or other documents that may be available electronically. On the other hand, they are not likely to fully digest large amounts of information and may select the wrong points unless the IT professional has carefully highlighted the most important issues.

It is also wise not to avoid reporters, since this will likely only motivate them to pursue the topic more vigorously. This is probably most true of student reporters on campus. They are part of the campus constituency, and it is wise to treat them with respect and courtesy. Remember that old adage by Mark Twain: "You should never pick a fight with a person who buys ink by the barrel." Talking with the media is a skill that nee ds to be developed, ideally in an a priori manner, before a crisis arises. During nonpressured times, the institutional public relations professionals can explain the desired behaviur for these situations. Also, in an excellent *EQ* article, Kandice Salomone and Paul Gandel provide a host of useful bits of advice in this arena.[3]

7. They Cultivate Their Advisory Committees

Advisory committees can be extraordinarily helpful to and an enormous ally of IT professionals, but they can also be a nightmare if not managed effectively. As with the other skills noted above, there is no defined curriculum for learning to work with advisory committees. First of all, though called advisory committees, in reality these groups are more about governance than advice. Committee members are the designated voice of key constituencies, and they need to be heeded. When posing key issues and questions to such groups, the IT professional needs to be prepared to do something with the information they provide or, at least, to explain why their advice has not been followed. Otherwise, they will eventually cease to participate meaningfully and will drop out; or, worse yet, they may become active adversaries. The IT professional should consider consulting with the chair and perhaps also a number of key members offline, not just when an official meeting is scheduled. This may seem Machiavellian, but it is important to take advantage of the power of these governance structures. This means cultivating the relationships and making sure the committee members are well-informed emissaries for the committee's function.

Generally, the advisory committee is not a working group. Its purpose is to help define direction and policy—not to do the work of the IT service unit or to act as the de facto manager of this unit. The committee members need to know what they are to do and need to have a clear mandate or charge, which probably cannot be repeated too many times. They need to know that governance is not management and that their responsibilities are directional, not operational. For the IT professional, this means setting some clear boundaries, without in any way intimating that the committee members need to mind their own business. Ideally such committees will reflect the breadth of the campus. All too often such groups are populated by zealots who may have in-depth knowledge but who are also likely to have particular axes to grind. Representation of the general campus and of the needs of various academic or administrative sectors is a much preferred approach. For more on this topic, William H. Pritchard has written an excellent *EQ* article that summarizes some very good advice regarding campus advisory committees.[4]

8. They Are Enablers

The goals of any organizational leader in a service role, whether in IT or not, should be to enable others to accomplish their goals. All IT professionals are ultimately in the "service" business—assisting students, faculty, and staff to achieve their goals, since IT is ultimately a means to an end and not an end in and of itself. The job of the IT professional is to help others on campus figure out how the information or the technology can allow them to better serve the missions of their units and, ultimately, the campus. This can be accomplished more effectively if the IT professional is perceived as assisting and acting in partnership with the end user. Many of the suggestions in this [chapter] are intended to assist the IT professional in better understanding and better appreciating the problems faced by these end users. On the other hand, the IT professional needs to be careful not to create the impression that he or she understands the problem as well as or better than the end users, who have spent their careers in a particular area of expertise. The IT professional needs to be a partner and to avoid stepping on the toes of those who are ultimately responsible for a given area.

9. They Don't Whine

At one time or another, everyone has felt beaten down and frustrated by the demands, changing directions, and perceived injustices of the organizational existence. This is natural, not at all uncommon, and simply part of living and participating in the social organizational structure of the college or university. We may not agree with some new directions being taken. We may think a boss is stupid. We may feel that some things are not fair and should not have occurred. The challenge that all of us face is how we go about combatting or reacting to these situations.

An all-too-common method for dealing with such things is to whine. Whining diminishes the whiner and seldom accomplishes anything constructive. Whiners—who talk incessantly about how bad things are, why things aren't fair, how terrible everything is, and how much better things are someplace else—do themselves and the whole organization a disservice. If things are bad and need changing, it is up to the IT professional to identify alternative courses of action, new directions, or different ways of doing more with less. If other options have been tried and these attempts rejected, and if the IT professional feels there is a greener pasture elsewhere, then he or she should go find it. Unfortunately, many whiners don't want to create new options. Others cannot move on. But if they stay and continue to whine, they need to realize that they are hurting the credibility of their unit, and potentially the whole organization, since other people in the organization will come to discount the whiners (and their units) even if they have a legitimate point. Such behavior gives the impression—or, perhaps, reinforces the reality—that this person and his or her unit is not a team player and is not trying to help the organization do its very best in difficult circumstances.

10. They Are Generalists

One of the challenges that IT professionals must face is that they enter their careers as specialists, with much of their professional identity and self-concept based on the fact that they are highly skilled and knowledgeable about a given, albeit limited, area of expertise. As they mature in the IT profession, they must give up some of the security that this specialized identity has provided and become more rounded, more of a generalist, in order to tackle problems that cut across specialized and professional boundaries and silos. As the IT professional moves up the organizational ladder, he or she must develop the mindset, the worldview, and the skills of a generalist in order to be successful. This isn't always comfortable, but it is essential. Being—and being perceived as—a member of the broader academic community, not just a niche player, gives a person standing and credibility in the decision-making process within any college or university.

In becoming generalists, IT professionals essentially blur the edges, making them less identifiable as a given "type" sitting at the table. If someone is perceived as a "techie" or a librarian and reinforces those stereotypes, that person is likely to be anticipated and potentially dismissed, since the other decision-makers may think that he or she is bringing a single mindset and perspective to the table. IT professionals need to break out of these stereotypes, drawing on some of the suggestions previously identified in this [chapter], in order to enhance both their personal credibility and the credibility of their units.

11. They Redefine Themselves

When IT professionals begin their careers, they likely define themselves as a systems programmer, or a security specialist, or an environmental biologist, or a reference librarian. Over time, this may evolve into a somewhat more generic term, such as "I'm an IT professional" or "I'm a librarian." But if we define ourselves in the silo of our technical or professional training, we are pushing an agenda in advancing that point of view or that particular solution or set of resources. Instead, we should all strive to be "people in support of the academic enterprise." This self-definition suggests that IT professionals consider themselves to be partners in the overall mission of the college or university. It means that they work hard not as advocates of a particular solution, but as partners supporting those with whom they work in achieving learning and discovery goals. This will be reflected in the extent to which others see them as a partner, a collaborator, and a co-conspirator. And finally, if IT professionals have accomplished all of this without being (or appearing to be) selfish and greedy, working as members of the broader institutional team, then they will be perceived as *responsible members of the academic enterprise*— the ultimate objective!

12. They Maintain Balance

I am often asked my thoughts on whether one can be a successful professional in the complex and demanding field of IT and also still have a personal life. I firmly believe this is possible, but as with so many of the other habits or skills discussed above, doing so requires planning and prioritization. It is unrealistic to expect that one can be a successful IT professional, pursue all of one's avocational activities and sports, have a full family life, and have time to watch all of the current television shows. It just doesn't work that way. The CIO position can easily consume fifty-five to eighty hours per week, especially if one tries to keep up with professional reading, block out time for thinking and planning, etc. As in everything else in life, there are trade-offs.

I can say from personal experience, however, that you can pursue a successful IT career and have a solid family life as well. I never missed my kids' soccer games or felt they were getting short shrift, and I have been happily married to the same lady for closing in on four decades. On the other hand, I have had little time myself for sports or leisure. I am not advocating this choice; I'm simply saying what worked for me. Each person has to make tough decisions, because it isn't possible to have it all. I also have found out that it is easy to start to slip and give work too much importance and time, rather than keeping this equation nicely balanced. Constant monitoring and adjustment are necessary.

Conclusion

The 12 habits presented in this chapter involve objectives and skills that seem apt for all IT professionals. Some of the skills are simple, but some take time and maturity to fully comprehend. Many of us who are current IT leaders wish we had picked up all of these habits earlier in our careers. We all need to work hard at growing constantly, no matter what age we are or what career stage we are in. Leadership occurs at numerous levels in a college or university, and everyone needs to develop personal growth and professional development plans to continue to improve as managers and as individuals. In addition, those of us who have been blessed with the job of supervising others in the IT field have the significant responsibility of helping those who work for and around us to acquire these skills, to turn these skills into habits—and thus to become successful IT professionals.

Endnotes

1. This [chapter] was developed from a presentation given to the Frye Leadership Institute, and later to the EDUCAUSE Leadership Institute, about the skills needed by a CIO to "play effectively" while sitting on the president's cabinet or the provost's council.

2. David Ward and Brian L. Hawkins, "Presidential Leadership for Information Technology," *EDUCAUSE Review*, vol. 38, no. 3 (May/June 2003), pp. 36–47, <http://www.educause.edu/LibraryDetailPage/666?ID=ERM0332>.

3. Kandice L. Salomone and Paul B. Gandel, "Talking with the Press," *EDUCAUSE Quarterly*, vol. 27, no. 2 (2004), pp. 61–65, <http://www.educause.edu/LibraryDetailPage/666?ID=EQM0427>.

4. William H. Pritchard, "Advice for IT Advisory Committees," *EDUCAUSE Quarterly*, vol. 28, no. 1 (2005), pp. 52–53, <http://www.educause.edu/LibraryDetailPage/666?ID=EQM0516>.

About the Author

Brian L. Hawkins is president of EDUCAUSE. Previously he was CIO and later senior vice president for academic planning and administrative affairs at Brown University. Prior to that, he was associate vice president for academic affairs at Drexel University. Hawkins is a management professor by training and the author of three books and many articles on organizational behavior and technology and academic planning. He received a PhD from Purdue University and bachelor's and master's degrees from Michigan State University.

CHAPTER 9

Cultivating People

Lida Larsen and Cynthia Golden
EDUCAUSE

According to Peter Senge, learning organizations are "organizations where people continually expand their capacity to create the results they truly desire, where new and expansive patterns of thinking are nurtured, where collective aspiration is set free, and where people are continually learning to see the whole together."[1] An important part of creating a true learning organization, in which we would all feel appreciated and fulfilled, is fostering a culture and environment where our employees are supported and valued and where they see themselves as an integral part of the institution. The authors who contributed to this book have clearly outlined the roles that both our higher education organizations and individual staff can play in creating a culture of continuous learning.

The effectiveness of our organizations ultimately depends on our people. Building an organization that people want to be part of and want to support requires that we place a strong emphasis on individual and staff development. "It is the dedication, motivation, knowledge, and skill sets of individuals that make a tremendous difference in the organization" is what Marilu Goodyear, Kathleen Ames-Oliver, and Keith Russell told us in chapter 3. They stressed the importance of heeding Marcus Buckingham's proposal that the phrase "Get People Done Through Work" should be our motto. No matter how we state it, we should recognize that our people are fundamental to our organizations' health and success, and cultivating our people is our responsibility. It also makes good sense.

The Times, They Are A-Changin' (Again)

Many of the authors in this book began their careers when organizations tended to be paternalistic and hierarchical, and Bob Dylan was singing about a world in transition. Our first ideas of work may have been flavored by our parents and their memories of the Great Depression. Many of their generation believed one should look for a good job near home and cling to it, because workers were expendable. A stable job with good pay was important. Getting ahead meant working longer hours, "not rocking the boat," and silently hoping for a raise or a promotion. The GI Bill provided a new avenue to higher education, and a college education became important in order to "get ahead." On-the-job skills training was available, but professional development in the workplace, as described in this book, was rare.

Things have changed significantly over the past 50 to 60 years. In chapter 1, James Bruce and Brian McDonald led us through our recent history, showing how we have moved from an era when our leaders were technologists placed in leadership roles—people who simply "got technology projects done"—to today's environment of leaders who are higher education professionals and technology integrators who must understand the business of higher education to focus on complex client services. They wrote, "IT leaders need to evolve as the context continues to change." We are undeniably in transition to an age where collaboration, flattening organizational structures, recognition of the individual, and appreciation of the value of staff and professional development have become increasingly important as we compete in an ever-widening global marketplace. We need to prepare our organizations for continual change—to move to an undefined future where the only thing we know is that the model will change again, probably more frequently. "We live in a very dynamic higher education ecosystem where adaptation has become the norm," said Gene Spencer and Jeannie Zappe in chapter 2. A fundamental assumption here is that we will each have several different types of jobs in multiple organizations during our careers.

Change is the byword. Whether we supervise longtime staff or new recruits, it is our job to help them develop the skills and self-confidence they will need not only to be flexible and adaptable but to be change agents themselves as they participate in the ever-evolving world of technology in higher education.

Building the Higher Education IT Workforce
How do we find and develop talented people who will provide transformational leadership at all levels of our organizations? If we identify them, will they want to work for us? We compete directly with other sectors of society for the best and the brightest talent. How marketable are our organizations to the people we want on our teams? What are the unique reasons someone would want to work in higher education? Tracey Leger-Hornby and Ron Bleed suggested in chapter 7 that factors include the collegial atmosphere, built-in services, learning

opportunities, the nonprofit mission, and the opportunity to contribute back to the community, thus making a difference. "Making a difference," said William Hogue and David Dodd in chapter 4, may be the greatest personal measure of career success for some people.

Once we have the right people, what processes do we need to have in place to help them grow professionally and transfer knowledge within our workforce? How do we retain our intellectual capital within higher education? How do we capture the experience and wisdom of our leaders as they move on to other positions or retirement? As cited in several previous chapters, the 2004 ECAR study *Information Technology Leadership in Higher Education: The Condition of the Community*[2] found that a significant number of our current leaders will retire in the next few years, and we do not have staff in the pipeline interested in replacing them. How do we convey to younger, newer staff the importance of shared leadership for our organizations? How do we structure leadership positions so that new generations will find them of value and interest? If we haven't been thinking about these issues before, now is the time.

Knowing Who We Want—Technical Skills and Understanding

Each organization needs to think carefully about the attributes it seeks in the next-generation workforce and leaders. Many will be hired because they have specific technical skills needed to implement, maintain, and explain both the new and old systems the enterprise relies on each day. They will also need to be able to thrive in new organizational models and be predisposed to leadership roles. The authors in this book have offered a few ideas of the characteristics to look for in individuals as we build our organizations:

▶ **Continuous learner**—self-motivated, curious, agile, creative, a quick study, and open to new ideas

▶ **Communicator**—an empathetic listener and communication manager; both hears and conveys important information at all stakeholder levels and with a positive attitude

▶ **Collaborator**—service-oriented and stakeholder-motivated; also a negotiator, consensus builder, facilitator, and project manager

▶ **Change agent/manager**—understands the complexity of the enterprise, sees the big picture, is values driven, has character, is adaptable, and is willing to take risks

▶ **Competent**—organized, adaptable, and accountable people who understand technology and understand people

▶ **Centered**—serious about self-assessment and reflection, understand themselves and their own skills, and know when to turn to others

Competing for Talent

Where can we find people with these attributes? We don't have a long line of candidates standing at our doors vying for positions today. Computer and information science school enrollments are down, which means we have fewer recent graduates in the pipeline for our available jobs. And, it's not just higher education IT that's facing a shortage of the "right" people to join our profession: We are competing with industry, government, medicine, and other sectors for our next-generation workforce and leadership. They, too, say that they want skilled technology graduates with business acumen and the ability to see and understand the larger view of their increasingly complex environments and missions. Sitting back and waiting for the right people to come to us will not lead to success, especially when we know that other sectors have more resources for the recruitment process than we do. We need to put on our competitive hats and think of new ways to recruit, grow, and retain talented people to higher education. As Bruce and McDonald wrote in chapter 1, "One of the most important jobs any leader has is to develop the next generation of leaders." We must tackle this responsibility proactively and with vigor.

Campus Efforts

Whether you have long-standing, institutionalized organizational and professional development programs or are just starting to think about possibilities, you can take important steps to make sure your efforts succeed.

▶ **Start setting expectations before you hire.** Don't make your programs an afterthought. Spencer and Zappe suggested in chapter 2 that we should focus on organizational and professional development issues in the recruitment and hiring process in order to set the stage for expectations and commitments from both the organization and the individual. Bucknell uses this approach along with conversations and concerted efforts to continually reshape their organization and provide the professional development resources to keep individuals a vital part of the team.

▶ **Create a diverse workforce.** The value of multiple perspectives and styles in decision making is well known. Many of us have taken Myers-Briggs Type Indicator (MBTI) and other kinds of assessments to help us better understand ourselves and how we best communicate and work with others. Whatever you believe about the value of the specific category assignments, these exercises show, in a very understandable way, why diversity is important as we develop organizations with shared leadership. Keep in mind that the skills you seek may be found outside the traditional realm of IT, whether in higher education or other environments. IT staff don't all need to be techies. Many examples show nontechnical people providing exemplary leadership in the field. Whether they began their working lives as a lawyer, ornithologist, MBA, librarian, or women's studies professor, they may have just the skills you need as you diversify your staff. Hire student interns and grow them to be future employees in your organization. Set aside part of the budget for this purpose.

▶ **Imagine new time and work models.** We are already faced with providing 24 x 7 services that call for time and work models other than traditional nine-to-five jobs. Flexible scheduling, job sharing, and working remotely are just a few of the ways we can offer options to our staff. We can also look into collaborations with other departments and institutions with opportunities for joint products or services and cross-training as we move into areas not traditionally considered technical.

▶ **Market the higher education workplace—and your organization.** Some organizations have strong public relations and marketing programs for both the products of the organization and for employment and retention. For our purposes, we should think more broadly about how to market to those who have never considered a career in higher education. We must market higher education mission and benefits routinely—not just on special occasions or when we need to hire a new person. We should think of ourselves as ambassadors for the higher education workplace everywhere we go. Be intentional about speaking up for higher education and IT in higher education. Here are some starter ideas:

  ▷ Join your region's "technology council" and meet your peers in other sectors—this is a great way to get the word out about IT at your institution.

  ▷ Work with your public affairs or media relations office and learn how and when to deliver your message.

  ▷ Always have the "three-minute elevator speech" ready and use it when appropriate. Be able to talk about your organization, key things happening there, and available or upcoming opportunities.

  ▷ Participate in the annual campus community open house and let the community know how you contribute to your institution.

▷ Know your message. What would attract someone to higher education as a place to work? You might mention the collegial environment, adequate benefits, historically valued mission (both institutional and global), clearly articulated expectations, appropriate resources, clear rewards and accountability, partnership in leadership and decision making, opportunities for creativity, opportunities for growth (technical, management, and leadership), a flexible and collaborative workplace, and work that matters. Don't forget tuition remission, campus recreation center facilities, fine arts center and programs, intellectual growth opportunities with daily seminars and library privileges, and other perks. And finally, stress the cachet of belonging to the higher education enterprise. A good resource is the American Council on Education's Solutions for Our Future program (http://www.solutionsforourfuture.org/).

The Role of Professional Development in Retention

As Stanley Davis and Christopher Meyer wrote in *Blur*, "It isn't a sustainable course to ignore your people's development needs. You'll only lose them faster that way—or never attract them in the first place."[3]

Spencer and Zappe affirmed that a strong learning and growth environment is a key factor in staff retention. Deliberate, formal professional development, as covered in this book, with coaching, mentoring, cross-training, and assignments that stretch individuals' abilities, organizational support for individual and organizational assessment, on-the-job opportunities for active learning and distributed leadership, and more, show that you care about individuals and their contributions to the organization.

Bruce and McDonald suggested in chapter 1 that creating career ladders for those who don't aspire to senior leadership positions can be an important way to provide opportunities for non-CIO-track staff to share in leadership roles. It's also a way to increase the likelihood that an individual will want to stay on staff. Most of us know of people who moved into management or leadership roles in order to get a promotion and raise and in so doing left behind a position in which they were superbly competent and happy. Once unhappily established in the new position, it's easier to move outside the organization than to return to the original job.

Creating work environments that are "friendly" for families, women, part-time students, or other groups like new hires from the Net Generation can be critical in retaining staff. We all know competent, experienced people who have resigned from positions because the work environment was not flexible enough to permit them to care for family members, be it a new baby, an aging parent, or a spouse with a long-term illness. Many people who want to be an integral part of our staff can balance family or school issues quite well if given options for flexible scheduling. Leger-Hornby and Bleed addressed a number of these issues in chapter 7, and Joanne Kossuth and Leger-Hornby wrote a good resource for attracting and retaining women to organizations.[4]

While it is important for the organization to do all it can to create an environment that fosters personal and professional growth, it is also important for the individual to take responsibility for his or her own professional development and future. In chapter 6 Golden and Updegrove discuss why professional activity is important to one's career and offer suggestions to the employee about strategies for getting involved at all levels.

Finally, it is important to understand that allowing good staff to move on to other opportunities not only benefits the person, it strengthens the profession. Balancing institutional interests with individual career paths is a well-accepted practice in higher education. Each new role in our careers, and each new institution we work for, contributes to our broader perspectives and helps us become more valuable as employees. Each job should prepare us for the next one.

The Next Generation of Leaders

This book has paid special attention to cultivating the next generation of leaders in the IT and information resource arena. The anticipated retirement of large numbers of those in senior leadership positions is cause for concern and requires proactive measures to ensure continuity and avoid the loss of institutional knowledge during the transition. At some institutions, formal programs address this problem by identifying emerging leaders, providing them with opportunities to observe leaders in action and allowing them to participate in leadership experiences. Georgia Tech's Master's Series program was created "to identify and develop the leadership skills of selected candidates to build 'bench strength' for senior leaders on the Georgia Tech campus as well as meet the institute's need to grow, develop, and retain future leaders,"[5] and the university's Office of Information Technology's Professional Leaders program builds on that experience for IT professionals. In chapter 5, Metros and Yang discussed the role mentoring can play in preparing the next generation. In chapter 8, Brian Hawkins recommended developing skills early in one's career that will become habits of the successful IT professional.

Having plans in place before some of the more seasoned executives move onward is critical. New leaders may not come from our current IT workforce, however. Examining other potential sources of leadership talent, including faculty, administrators, and others on campus who have a solid understanding of IT, as well as recruiting from the corporate world may be useful strategies toward building the leadership pool.

Current IT Staff: Are They Ready?

Campus IT staff possess significant talent that should be poised for leadership at many different levels. While a few potential leaders will rise to the top, the ECAR study indicates that most do not aspire to formal leadership roles.[6] Some may have begun their careers with us as part-time student employees and simply found it a comfortable place to stay. Some may find their energy in having their hands on the technology, not in working with people. Some may see leadership and management roles as stressful and demanding time they are unwilling to give. Some do not possess the confidence that they can do the job when indeed they can. It behooves us to model appropriate time management and shared responsibility in such a way that these are not concerns for potential leaders. We can plant the seeds for shared leadership in all of our people, but we cannot force it. In chapter 2, Spencer and Zappe suggested that when we see good candidates for leadership roles, we take advantage of "opportunistic evolution," moving forward when people are ready and steering them toward leadership positions in an evolutionary, nonthreatening way. For others, we need to make sure they still have opportunities for professional development and growth on a nonmanagement career ladder that recognizes technical achievement.

Looking to Your Campus Colleagues

You don't need to convince people on your campus that your institution is a great place to work. Most people are there because they believe strongly in the mission of higher education. They already consider themselves higher education professionals. People who could contribute substantially to the IT group may not be IT professionals, however. Faculty, administrators, and others may have great insight into technology use. We might already be working with these people on collaborative projects. They may be contributing as leaders on our IT advisory committees. Or, they might be ignoring us—moving ahead with innovative ideas on their own. Whatever their current positions, they may be strong candidates to join our teams. Some may be interested in a full shift to IT leadership, while others might be interested in a program that allows them to join the IT staff on a temporary basis, for six months or a year, or on a part-time basis. These approaches may be valuable experiences for both the non-IT person and the IT staff.

Reaching Outside the Gates

We need to discover new and creative ways to find, reach, and connect with candidates from outside higher education. As the ECAR study indicates, new campus IT staff hired from industry probably will need help acclimating to the culture and politics of a higher education organization.[7] This seems a small concession in obtaining valuable talent. We lose people to the corporate world and other sectors generally for more salary and financial benefits—and because they might not have realized that a position in higher education was viable for them. But who is to say that there aren't people in industry who'd like to move in the other direction and are willing to take a smaller salary in exchange for the collegial environment? How do we find them? Imagine new places to search, and search continuously. Develop professional relationships outside higher education, and don't hesitate to circulate key position openings within these communities.

While many institutions have set guidelines for searches and job ad placement, their ultimate goal is to help you find the people you need. Make human resources staff your partners in designing streamlined job searches that reach a wider, yet targeted, audience.[8]

Knowing the right person at the right time might well help you fill a position. This is where keeping in touch with others professionally and involving them in the life of your enterprise can provide a huge benefit. A few examples of ways you might do this follow.

▶ Pay attention to your contacts and collaborators from the outside. Vendors sometimes find higher education attractive, and colleagues at other institutions may be looking for a change of pace.

▶ Routinely bring outside people in via seminars and similar professional events and let them experience, though briefly, what it's like to be on a campus.

▶ The Intergovernmental Personnel Act (http://www.opm.gov/programs/ipa/) is a government program for loaning employees to other institutions for a year. It can provide a good introduction to the higher education environment for them, and vice versa.

▶ Reread the marketing section above.

Harvesting Institutional Knowledge

While it seems clear that we must concentrate on bringing new talent and perspectives into our organizations, it also seems clear that we have a great opportunity to continue productive relationships with those who may soon be looking to step down from their current management and leadership roles. Models exist for continuing these relationships and making effective transfers of knowledge that can work well for us in higher education.

We can "borrow back" expertise and leadership by finding part-time or job-sharing roles for those who do not wish to fully retire but would prefer to cut back their hours while continuing to work and contribute to the enterprise. Pairing these individuals with newer staff provides an opportunity for mentoring and for transfer of knowledge and perspective. Formal programs for knowledge transfer can begin long before actual retirement. One Southwestern institution paired an aspiring CIO with the retiring CIO for a full year of collaboration. It was a successful partnership, and the CIO job was awarded to the apprentice.

The American Association of Retired People (AARP) reported that a strong majority of seniors want flexible work arrangements over daily, weekly, and even seasonal timeframes. CVS/pharmacy lets their snowbirds (people who travel south in the winter) work seasonally in different locations and for flexible hours. That might seem a bit of a stretch for the higher education environment, but with the ability to work from remote locations and similar situations, it could be a win-win option for some. Imagine a college in the North arranging a shared position with a university in the South, for example.

Whether through phased retirement, buying consulting time from retirees, or other creative transition techniques, it is important that we recognize that not only history but real institutional knowledge leaves along with our colleagues. It should be harvested and disseminated throughout the organization whenever possible.

Looking Ahead

In his address to the Seminars on Academic Computing in 2005, George O. Strawn, CIO at the National Science Foundation, spoke about change being the "constant of modern times."[9] Those of us in higher education have been actively engaged in developing, managing, and applying more technological change during our careers than previous generations have seen in their lifetimes. Many of the authors of this book were themselves part of creating the IT culture in which we work today. What we can draw from their writings is the primacy of people to the development of solutions for our future. If we don't care for ourselves and our colleagues, develop skills and career paths, or mentor future leaders, our institutions will not thrive, we will not fulfill our responsibilities to society, and we won't be very happy.

Rather than conclude this chapter, and this book, we prefer to look toward the future we are helping to build. Margaret J. Wheatley captured our imagination in the introduction to the second edition of her *Leadership and the New Science: Discovering Order in a Chaotic World*:

> I believe the fundamental work of this time—work that requires the participation of all of us—is to discover new ways of being together. Our old ways of relating to each other don't support us any longer, whether it's at home, in community, at work, or as nation states... We are all pioneers and discoverers of a new world, and we all need one another. It is up to us to journey forth in search of new practices and new ideas that will enable us to create lives and organizations worthy of human habitation.[10]

Endnotes

1. Peter Senge, *The Fifth Discipline: The Art and Practice of the Learning Organization* (New York: Doubleday, 1990).

2. Richard N. Katz et al., *Information Technology Leadership in Higher Education: The Condition of the Community* (Boulder, Colo.: EDUCAUSE Center for Applied Research, research study, vol. 1, 2004), <http://www.educause.edu/LibraryDetailPage/666?ID=ERS0401>.

3. Stanley M. Davis and Christopher Meyer, *Blur* (Cambridge, Mass.: Perseus Books, 1998).

4. Joanne Kossuth and Tracey Leger-Hornby, "Attracting Women to Technical Professions," *EDUCAUSE Quarterly*, vol. 27, no. 3 (2004), pp. 46–49, <http://www.educause.edu/LibraryDetailPage/666?ID=EQM0435>.

5. Linda A. Cabot, "Professional Development for IT Leaders," *EDUCAUSE Quarterly*, vol. 29, no. 1 (2006), pp. 54–56, <http://www.educause.edu/ir/library/pdf/eqm0619.pdf>.

6. Katz et al., op. cit.

7. Ibid.

8. For a description of two IT recruiting efforts, see "IT Recruiting—Great Candidates Can Be Found," a presentation at EDUCAUSE 2000 by Judy Caruso and Jennifer Gebert, <http://www.educause.edu/ir/library/pdf/EDU0034.pdf>; and "Streamlining the Recruitment Process in a State University," by Lida L. Larsen, Linda Gilday, and Terry

Moore, presented at the 29th Annual ACM SIGUCCS Conference on User Services in 2001, <http://portal.acm.org/citation.cfm?id=500956.501017>.

9. George O. Strawn, "Change: The Constant of Modern Times," presentation at the 2005 Seminars on Academic Computing, Snowmass, Colorado, <http://www.educause.edu/LibraryDetailPage/666?ID=SAC0503>.

10. Margaret J. Wheatley, ed., *Leadership and the New Science: Discovering Order in a Chaotic World, 2nd Edition* (San Francisco: Berrett-Koehler Publishers, 1999).

About the Authors

Lida Larsen is a professional development specialist at EDUCAUSE, supporting regional conference programming and PD activity development. She previously served as vice chair and conference liaison for the ACM Special Interest Group for University and College Computing Services (SIGUCCS). Since 1968, she has held educational, management, and leadership roles in K-12, Prince George's Community College, and the University of Maryland. At Maryland, she received their first annual Outstanding Student Employer of the Year Award. Larsen received her master's of library science from the University of Maryland and her BA in educational media from Purdue University.

Cynthia Golden is a vice president of EDUCAUSE. She is responsible for EDUCAUSE's professional development activities as well as the association's e-content and knowledge management initiatives, and has general oversight of information technology services and strategies within the association. She previously held IT management and leadership positions at Carnegie Mellon University, MIT, and Duquesne University. She holds a BA from Indiana University of Pennsylvania and an MS from the University of Pittsburgh.

Index

EDUCAUSE

Transforming Education Through Information Technologies

info@educause.edu

1150 18th Street, NW, Suite 1010

Washington, DC 20036

202-872-4200

202-872-4318 (fax)

www.educause.edu

4772 Walnut Street, Suite 206

Boulder, CO 80301

303-449-4430

303-440-0461 (fax)